Volume IX
Report No. 92
January 1975

D1298722

The Educated Woman: Prospects and Problems

Formulated by the
Committee on the College Student

Group for the Advancement of Psychiatry

This publication was produced for the Group for the Advancement of Psychiatry by the Mental Health Materials Center, Inc., New York.

Additional copies of this GAP Publication No. 92 are available at the following prices: 1–9 copies, $4.00 each; 10–24 copies, list less 15 per cent; 25–99 copies, list less 20 per cent; 100–499 copies, list less 30 per cent.

Upon request the Publications Office of the Group for the Advancement of Psychiatry will provide a complete listing of GAP titles currently in print, quantity prices, and information on subscriptions assuring the receipt of new publications as they are released.

Orders amounting to less than $5.00 must be accompanied by remittance. All prices are subject to change without notice.

Please send your order and remittance to: Publications Office, Group for the Advancement of Psychiatry, 419 Park Avenue South, New York, New York 10016.

Standard Book Number 87318–129-8
Library of Congress Catalog Card Number 62-2872
Printed in the United States of America

TABLE OF CONTENTS

This is the second in a series of publications comprising Volume IX. For a list of other GAP publications on topics of current interest, please see last page of book herein.

STATEMENT OF PURPOSE

THE GROUP FOR THE ADVANCEMENT OF PSYCHIATRY has a membership of approximately 300 psychiatrists, most of whom are organized in the form of a number of working committees. These committees direct their efforts toward the study of various aspects of psychiatry and the application of this knowledge to the fields of mental health and human relations.

Collaboration with specialists in other disciplines has been and is one of GAP's working principles. Since the formation of GAP in 1946 its members have worked closely with such other specialists as anthropologists, biologists, economists, statisticians, educators, lawyers, nurses, psychologists, sociologists, social workers, and experts in mass communication, philosophy, and semantics. GAP envisages a continuing program of work according to the following aims:

1. To collect and appraise significant data in the fields of psychiatry, mental health, and human relations
2. To reevaluate old concepts and to develop and test new ones
3. To apply the knowledge thus obtained for the promotion of mental health and good human relations

GAP is an independent group, and its reports represent the composite findings and opinions of its members only, guided by its many consultants.

THE EDUCATED WOMAN: PROSPECTS AND PROBLEMS *was formulated by the Committee on the College Student, which acknowledges on page 116 the participation of former Committee members in preparation of this report. The current members of this committee, as well as other committees, and the officers of GAP are listed below.*

COMMITTEE ON THE COLLEGE STUDENT
Robert L. Arnstein, Hamden, Conn., Chr.
Harrison P. Eddy, New York
Malkah Tolpin Notman, Brookline, Mass.

Gloria C. Onque, Pittsburgh
Kent E. Robinson, Towson, Md.
Earle Silber, Chevy Chase, Md.
Tom G. Stauffer, White Plains, N.Y.

Frederick Gottlieb, Bel Air, Calif.
Benjamin Jeffries, Harper Woods, Mich.
Ruth W. Lidz, Woodbridge, Conn.
Mary E. Mercer, Nyack, N.Y.
Harris B. Peck, Bronx, N.Y.
Marvin E. Perkins, White Plains, N.Y.

COMMITTEE ON PSYCHIATRY AND LAW
Carl P. Malmquist, Minneapolis, Chr.
Edward T. Auer, St. Louis
John Donnelly, Hartford
Peter Browning Hoffman, Charlottesville
A. Louis McGarry, Brookline, Mass.
Seymour Pollack, Los Angeles
Loren H. Roth, Rockville, Md.
Gene L. Usdin, New Orleans

COMMITTEE ON PSYCHIATRY AND RELIGION
Sidney Furst, Bronx, N.Y., Chr.
Stanley A. Leavy, New Haven
Richard C. Lewis, New Haven
Albert J. Lubin, Woodside, Calif.
Mortimer Ostow, Bronx, N.Y.
Bernard L. Pacella, New York
Michael R. Zales, Greenwich, Conn.

COMMITTEE ON PSYCHIATRY AND THE
COMMUNITY
Alexander S. Rogawski, Los Angeles, Chr.
C. Knight Aldrich, Charlottesville, Va.
Herbert C. Modlin, Topeka
John C. Nemiah, Boston
Charles B. Wilkinson, Kansas City, Mo.

COMMITTEE ON PSYCHIATRY IN INDUSTRY
Herbert L. Klemme, Topeka, Chr.
Thomas L. Brannick, Imola, Calif.
Duane Q. Hagen, St. Louis
R. Edward Huffman, Asheville, N.C.
Alan A. McLean, New York
David E. Morrison, Topeka
Clarence J. Rowe, St. Paul
John Wakefield, Los Gatos, Calif.

COMMITTEE ON PSYCHOPATHOLOGY
Charles Shagass, Philadelphia, Chr.
Aaron T. Beck, Wynnewood, Pa.
Wagner H. Bridger, Bronx, N.Y.
Paul E. Huston, Iowa City
Richard E. Renneker, Los Angeles
George E. Ruff, Philadelphia

Albert J. Silverman, Ann Arbor, Mich.
George E. Vaillant, Cambridge, Mass.

COMMITTEE ON PUBLIC EDUCATION
Miles F. Shore, Boston, Chr.
Leo H. Bartemeier, Baltimore
Mildred Mitchell Bateman, Charleston
Robert J. Campbell, New York
James A. Knight, New Orleans
John P. Lambert, Katonah, N.Y.
Norman L. Loux, Sellersville, Pa.
Peter A. Martin, Southfield, Mich.
Mabel Ross, Chicago
Julius Schreiber, Washington, D.C.
Robert H. Sharpley, Cambridge, Mass.
Robert A. Solow, Beverly Hills
Kent A. Zimmerman, Berkeley

COMMITTEE ON RESEARCH
Morris A. Lipton, Chapel Hill, Chr.
Stanley E. Eldred, Belmont, Mass.
Donald F. Klein, Glen Oaks, N.Y.
Ralph R. Notman, Brookline, Mass.
Alfred H. Stanton, Wellesley Hills, Mass.
Eberhard H. Uhlenhuth, Chicago

COMMITTEE ON SOCIAL ISSUES
Roy W. Menninger, Topeka, Chr.
Viola W. Bernard, New York
Roderic Gorney, Los Angeles
Lester Grinspoon, Boston
Joel S. Handler, Evanston, Ill.
Judd Marmor, Los Angeles
Perry Ottenberg, Merion Station, Pa.
Kendon W. Smith, Piermont, N.Y.
Raymond G. Wilkerson, Chicago

COMMITTEE ON THERAPEUTIC CARE
Robert W. Gibson, Towson, Md., Chr.
Bernard Bandler, Boston
Thomas E. Curtis, Chapel Hill
Harold A. Greenberg, Silver Spring, Md
Milton Kramer, Cincinnati
Orlando B. Lightfoot, Boston
Melvin Sabshin, Chicago
Robert E. Switzer, Topeka

COMMITTEE ON THERAPY
Justin Simon, Berkeley, Chr.
Henry W. Brosin, Tucson, Ariz.
Peter H. Knapp, Boston

114

Eugene Meyer, Baltimore
Robert Michels, New York
Andrew P. Morrison, Cambridge
William C. Offenkrantz, Chicago
William L. Peltz, Manchester, Vt.
Franz K. Reichsman, Brooklyn
Lewis L. Robbins, Glen Oaks, N.Y.
Richard I. Shader, Newton Centre, Mass.
Harley C. Shands, New York
Joseph P. Tupin, Sacramento
Herbert Weiner, Bronx, N.Y.

CONTRIBUTING MEMBERS

Carlos C. Alden, Jr., Buffalo
Charlotte G. Babcock, Pittsburgh
Grace Baker, New York
Walter E. Barton, Washington, D. C.
Spencer Bayles, Houston, Tex.
Anne R. Benjamin, Chicago
Ivan C. Berlien, Coral Gables, Fla.
Sidney Berman, Washington, D. C.
Grete L. Bibring, Cambridge
Edward G. Billings, Denver
Carl A. L. Binger, Cambridge
H. Waldo Bird, St. Louis
Wilfred Bloomberg, Boston
H. Keith H. Brodie, Baltimore
Eugene Brody, Menlo Park, Calif.
Matthew Brody, Brooklyn, N.Y.
Ewald W. Busse, Durham
Dale Cameron, Guilford, Conn.
Gerald Caplan, Boston
Hugh T. Carmichael, Washington, D. C.
Ian L. W. Clancey, Maitland, Ont., Can.
Sanford I. Cohen, Boston
Jules V. Coleman, New Haven
Robert Coles, Cambridge
Frank J. Curran, New York
William D. Davidson, Washington, D. C.
Leonard J. Duhl, Berkeley
Lloyd C. Elam, Nashville
Joel Elkes, Baltimore
Joseph T. English, New York
Louis C. English, Pomona, N.Y.
O. Spurgeon English, Narberth, Pa.
Dana L. Farnsworth, Boston
Stuart M. Finch, Tucson, Ariz.
Alfred Flarsheim, Chicago
Archie R. Foley, New York
Alan Frank, Albuquerque, N. M.
Daniel X. Freedman, Chicago
Albert J. Glass, Chicago

Louis A. Gottschalk, Irvine, Calif.
Milton Greenblatt, Sepulveda, Calif.
Maurice H. Greenhill, Scarsdale, N. Y.
John H. Greist, Indianapolis
Roy R. Grinker, Sr., Chicago
Ernest M. Gruenberg, Poughkeepsie, N. Y.
Edward O. Harper, Cleveland, Ohio
Mary O'Neill Hawkins, New York
J. Cotter Hirschberg, Topeka
Edward J. Hornick, New York
Joseph Hughes, Philadelphia
Portia Bell Hume, Berkeley
Irene M. Josselyn, Phoenix
Jay Katz, New Haven
Sheppard G. Kellam, Chicago
Marion E. Kenworthy, New York
Gerald L. Klerman, Boston
Othilda M. Krug, Cincinnati
Zigmond M. Lebensohn, Washington, D. C.
Henry D. Lederer, Washington, D. C.
Robert L. Leopold, Philadelphia
Alan I. Levenson, Tucson, Ariz.
Earl A. Loomis, New York
Reginald S. Lourie, Washington, D. C.
Alfred O. Ludwig, Boston
Jeptha R. MacFarlane, Westbury, N. Y.
John A. MacLeod, Cincinnati
Sidney G. Margolin, Denver
Helen V. McLean, Chicago
Jack H. Mendelson, Belmont, Mass.
Karl A. Menninger, Topeka
James G. Miller, Louisville, Ky.
John A. P. Millet, Nyack, N. Y.
Peter B. Neubauer, New York
Rudolph G. Novick, Lincolnwood, Ill.
Lucy D. Ozarin, Bethesda, Md.
Irving Philips, San Francisco
Charles A. Pinderhughes, Boston
Eveoleen N. Rexford, Cambridge
Milton Rosenbaum, Bronx, N. Y.
W. Donald Ross, Cincinnati
Lester H. Rudy, Chicago
David S. Sanders, Beverly Hills
Kurt O. Schlesinger, San Francisco
Elvin V. Semrad, Boston
Calvin F. Settlage, Sausalito, Calif.
Benson R. Snyder, Cambridge
John P. Spiegel, Waltham, Mass.
Brandt F. Steele, Denver
Eleanor A. Steele, Denver
Rutherford B. Stevens, New York
Alan A. Stone, Cambridge, Mass.

COMMITTEE ACKNOWLEDGMENTS

The Committee is particularly grateful to our Consultants: Elga R. Wasserman and Joseph Katz contributed significantly to the writing of the report; Alice S. Rossi gave thoughtful and constructive criticism which was invaluable in the formative period, and Kenneth Keniston provided extraordinarily useful and penetrating editorial comment. We are also greatly indebted to two pairs of Ginsburg Fellows: Clay C. Whitehead and Marlin Mattson were extremely helpful in the stages of initial conception and early writing and Harris Rabinovich and Allan I. Bezan were equally helpful in the later stages of reorganizing and sharpening the focus of the report in its final form.

In the preparation of the manuscript we were greatly aided by the Maurice Falk Medical Fund, which contributed generously to the costs of manuscript reproduction, and by Philip B. Hallen, President of the Falk Fund, whose encouragement, advice and personal support were always available when needed.

The tedious chore of typing and proofreading draft revisions was cheerfully done by members of the Division of Mental Hygiene, Yale University Health Services clerical and administrative staff: Lucy Cunningham, Marie Meneely, Mary Petrini, Ann Bishop, Doris Shumway and Janet Rozen.

Finally, we would like to acknowledge our debt to Alfred Flarsheim, a Committee member for many years, who participated in the early formulation of the report but retired from the Committee before its completion.

1

INTRODUCTION

College women contemplating their futures are confronted by uncertainty, conflicting pressures, and often false expectations. In a recent article in a popular magazine one woman, describing her life immediately after college, said that she had gotten married, had a baby, gotten divorced and spent the next years "growing up." She commented that she felt "the sequence was wrong," and she hoped that the current generation of college women would not suffer the same difficulties.[1]

The past ten years reflect a period of rising concern and "raised consciousness" with regard to the role of women in the United States, the consequences of which may affect some of the most important patterns of living. The Committee on the College Student of the Group for the Advancement of Psychiatry was particularly aware of this problem and of the issues associated with it because on campuses generally there has been much discussion about women's future roles, opportunities and relationships, and as psychiatrists dealing with women students in clinical settings they found it was frequently a focus of concern. Consequently, it seemed appropriate to frame a report on the college woman and the problems she faces today.

In initial discussions of the topic, a good reference point seemed to be the college woman in her junior or senior year, who is in the throes of making decisions that will inevitably affect her entire future—in other words, the college woman contemplating how the pattern of her life after graduation

117

will develop with respect to career, work, marriage and family. Consider the rather poignant situation cited above of the woman who has had issues unresolved in college or shortly thereafter come back to haunt her fifteen years later. If she could somehow have been helped to change the sequence and do it "the right way around"—however that would be defined for her as an individual—it would clearly have been a valuable service in terms of both diminishing human suffering and encouraging personal fulfillment.

All members of this committee had seen women in college who were beset by genuine conflict and uncertainty about their future. Statement 1, although not a clinical example, describes one student's feelings:

> Having rejected the option of immediately continuing on in school, I have been feeling at times a dread which is close to paralyzing—for there seems to be a near-vacuum of available resources of guidance for women intending to go out into the world directly from Ivy, to support themselves.
>
> Ivy seems to foist a kind of guilt on one who chooses this option. I would tend to think that the guilt may be more strongly felt by women here, for the trite notion of *noblesse oblige* on the part of women here is not to be underestimated. It would seem that the bulk of the energies directed by Ivy at graduating seniors is toward helping them continue on in their education, and where energies are directed toward helping students find employment, it is an understatement to say that these opportunities are overwhelmingly male-oriented.
>
> Second point: A senior male friend of mine commented to me the other day, "If I'm going to be a policeman, I'm going to be chief of the police force—If I'm going to be a professor, I'm going to be an Ivy professor." *Ivy men largely leave here with the feeling that whatever they eventually undertake, they will be the leaders, at the top, in control, and accomplish something significant.* Whatever the emphasis on 1,000 male leaders per year, this type of indoctrination has an unmis-

takable corollary effect on their women counterparts. I feel
that it would be difficult for me to be truly happy in a career
position where there was no opportunity to exercise some
type of creative leadership. It is acceptable socially and
intellectually (indeed expected) that the woman graduate of
many colleges take a job as a junior editor with Harper &
Row or as a junior researcher for Time-Life—positions that
are often more skin than bones, both intellectually and
monetarily. But what does it mean for an Ivy woman to
"make it"?

Which leads to point number three: Are our role models
for "making it" to be, as they seem to have been thus far,
those of the men? Or will we be able to develop distinctive
goals and means of our own, as I believe we must? Many of
the women I know who graduated from Ivy last year are at
law schools, graduate schools, business schools—and many
of the reasons for their choices seem to be closely related to
wanting to "make it" as an Ivy man might "make it." I am not
denigrating the option of continuing school—I am simply
attempting to deal with the plausibility of other alternatives
for the near future. Those women I know who are out
holding jobs seem to be suffering a painful identity crisis:
"Should I be doing something more, something better? Is
this what my Ivy education had led me to?"

The statement describes some of the real discrepancies
between individual ambitions, the expectations of others, and
the realistic possibilities. It also reveals the uncertainties and
the burdens imposed by having choices. Often, the most that
could be done for such students was to try to help them clarify
the sources of their confusion, some of which were rooted in
conflicts within themselves and some of which represented an
accurate view of social conditions for women. Where there
were intrapsychic obstacles, Committee members are under
the impression that in many instances these were crucial in
limiting choice in a way they did not for men—for example,
the degree to which women are limited by conflict in relation

to success and achievement. Where social conditions were paramount, women had also to deal with the ambivalence of society toward women, and particularly women who seek careers. Many of these problems are inseparable from those of becoming adult generally, but in the Committee's opinion, women face specific problems which are particularly intense in this era of changing sex roles and family patterns.

Because of social stereotyping, the woman who considers a career involving a major commitment outside the home may feel challenged about her femininity. If, in addition, she wants to work during the childbearing years, this threat is heightened, and conflict often ensues. This conflict is further intensified by the emphasis which has been placed on the mother's remaining at home and acting as the central housekeeper in the family. It is often stated that qualified women are very willing to sacrifice career aspirations in favor of the goals of marriage and family. In part, this is the result of widespread social attitudes which imply that it is wrong to make any other kind of choice, a conclusion frequently justified on the basis of "the biologically determined character of women." These attitudes about the "appropriate" concerns of women are particularly strong in the United States, where they are reinforced daily by the media. Take, for example, the following TV commercial:

> "Mother, for a while this morning, I thought I wasn't cut out for married life. Hank was late for work and forgot his apricot juice and walked out without kissing me, and when I was all alone I started crying. But then the postman came with the sheets and towels you sent, that look like big bandana handkerchiefs, and you know what I thought? That those big red and blue handkerchiefs are for girls like me to dry their tears on so they can get busy and do what a housewife has to do. Throw open the windows and start getting the house ready, and the dinner, maybe clean the silver and put new geraniums in the box. Everything to be ready for him when he walks through the door."

The assumption that women should be exclusively loving wives and mothers is not restricted to television. It is more widely shared by teachers, parents and employers than one might anticipate, and exerts a tremendous impact on the way women view themselves, how they are raised, and what is expected of them. In many important respects, most people behave the way they are expected to behave. Women are raised to believe in their own inferiority and to accept a subordinate status in society. The dynamics may be similar to those of minority groups such as blacks, even though women are not numerically a minority. It is not surprising, then, that in the face of peer group pressures, cultural norms, parental training, and teachers' expectations women are so often in conflict about achievement in adult realms other than the home. In a recent study, college women were asked to rate a series of professional articles.[2] For the purpose of the experiment, identical sets of articles were attributed to male and female authors. The respondents consistently rated articles signed by men better in terms of style and content than the same articles attributed to women.

As the discussion progressed in committee, two points of agreement were reached: The first was that the report would focus on the process of commitment to a life plan in the broadest sense. Members would not restrict themselves to such problems as whether a woman could successfully function as both a wife and a professional, or which professions were most practical for a woman to consider. These problems would be considered, but only as part of the more basic dilemma. Second, any such report about women must also consider the role of men, because women cannot be isolated from their social context, which includes as one critical component the male-female relationship. If one partner in a dynamic balance changes, the other will of necessity change also. Case 1 illustrates this point:

> Heidi and Jim were living together. Both were students in the same college. Jim was planning to work for a while after

graduation, Heidi to attend graduate school. They did not feel prepared to get married. She looked forward to graduation, which had the symbolic meaning of freeing her from a domineering, controlling family.

Although Heidi and Jim knew that contraceptive counseling was available, they "never got around to" doing anything about it. Just before graduation Heidi realized she was pregnant. She felt enormous guilt and in conflict about what to do. She began to argue with Jim, was unable to complete her work, and became depressed. Although very much interested in the graduate English program to which she had been accepted, she felt that to put her work above a family would be "wrong."

Heidi felt caught between her conscious wish for independence from her family and autonomy in her relationship with Jim and her fear about what this would involve. She went to a counselor for help in deciding what to do. In the course of counseling she recognized that in part her pregnancy was a way of dealing with her fear of going out into the world (of graduate school). This led her to become aware of her deeper dependency wishes. These insights made it easier for her to defer marriage and decide to have an abortion. As she discussed some of these feelings with Jim, he recognized that he had encouraged her dependency because it increased his feeling of masculinity. Unconsciously he had wanted the pregnancy to prove to himself his ability to be a father, and for this reason did not urge an abortion, although he realized that it was the "sensible" course of action.

Eventually, when both Heidi and Jim felt more established emotionally, they found their relationship to be more solidly based.

Once the general topic had been decided upon, the Committee acknowledged in its own composition the reflection of a common professional situation. At that point it consisted of nine men and one woman, with two male consultants. To correct this situation at least partially, two female consultants and one female psychiatrist were invited to participate.* The report subsequently formulated aims to clarify some of the current problems besetting the educated woman and our society, and hopefully to provide information that may help individual college students sort out some of their conflicts and uncertainties.

REFERENCES

1. Jane O'Reilly. The View from My Bed, *Ms.* (April 1973).
2. Philip Goldberg. Are Women Prejudiced Against Women? *Trans-action* 5 (1968): 28-30.

* See Committee Acknowledgments preceding.

2

AN HISTORICAL PERSPECTIVE

The position of women in Western society emerged with special force, as "an issue" during the 1960's. This was not a sudden development, but had significant historical roots which in the United States can be traced back for at least 150 years. The attempt of women to achieve equality with men has progressed unevenly in a number of areas—sometimes gaining ground, sometimes making little headway; and it has been attended by varying degrees of resistance on the part of society at large.[1] Particular periods or foci of intense activity have been given specific names, like the Women's Suffrage movement, or the Women's Rights movement—movements which have been paralleled by, and often intertwined with, other movements designed to gain equality for disadvantaged groups. The 1960's witnessed an upsurge of concern and action by feminist groups commonly referred to as "Women's Liberation." It raised crucially important issues about the role and place of women in our society and inevitably had an impact on the campus. No comprehensive history can be given here, but a few remarks will provide some background and perspective for the current concerns of college women.

In European society, women sporadically held positions of power or prominence by virtue of birth (e.g., royalty in England), connections (e.g., often as mistresses of important men), or talent (e.g., writers in Victorian England), but the pioneer society of this country clearly viewed them as "the weaker, the inferior sex. Their position in marriage was distinctly subordinate—their chief duty being 'obedience' to their husbands. Their mental and moral capacities were rated well below those of men."[2] In most instances, laws were based on English models and women had few rights. For example, women were not allowed to own land or to vote. Their role in the family, however, had a kind of functional integration into the societal fabric that a later technology made less essential.

In an agrarian society men and women shared jointly in the economic and social life of the communities in which they lived. Women participated in the production of food, manufacture of clothing, care of the sick, teaching of the young, and management of the home. They performed a multitude of tasks beyond those of bearing and rearing children. Although they were not paid for these tasks, often the men were not paid either, in the sense of receiving a salary, but the product of the labor of the entire family was sold. Furthermore, in Colonial America the scarcity of women enhanced their value.

During the nineteenth century the industrial revolution, which created a host of transformations, vitally altered the living patterns of both men and women. It caused a gradual shift from agriculture to industrial labor for men that brought with it a move from the farm to the city. This change was marked by two developments: (1) Women could at times compete for jobs in industry; and (2) many traditionally homemade products were replaced by factory-produced goods or commercially processed foods. Thus, household tasks became less time-consuming for middle-class women, whose energy, freed for activities outside the home, was commandeered by education, volunteer work, jobs, political activity and social reform.[3] Opposed to this trend was the Victorian emphasis on the sanctity of the home and hearth "as the fount of all the tender virtues in life."[4] Women were installed as goddesses of the hearth, and while this gained them some reverence, it also confined them to the home.

Women and education

The fight for education for women progressed slowly. Not
until the latter part of the eighteenth century were secondary
schools available to girls. The admission of women to colleges
came later.[5] In the early part of the nineteenth century several
of the better women's seminaries provided an education ap-
proaching in quality that of men's colleges, and later some of
them attained collegiate rank—notably Mount Holyoke,
founded as a seminary in 1837. Oberlin College was years
ahead of the times in its encouragement of women, offering
them admission in 1837. But it was not until mid-century that
other colleges followed suit. In 1855, Elmira, and in 1865,
Vassar, were established as women's colleges, followed by
Smith, Wellesley and Bryn Mawr. In 1852, Antioch followed
Oberlin's lead and became coeducational, as did Cornell. The
passage in 1862 of the Land Grant Act, which authorized
grants of land for state agricultural colleges, and the subsequent strengthening of state universities, considerably increased the opportunities for women because most state universities were coeducational from the beginning or became so
rather rapidly. In the latter part of the century several
women's colleges (Pembroke, Jackson, Barnard, Radcliffe)
were opened as affiliates of established men's colleges.

Although by 1900 some progress had been made by women
in attaining a college education, their admission to the professions was in general further delayed.[6] Elizabeth Blackwell,
later hailed as the first woman physician, obtained a medical
degree against odds from Geneva Medical College in 1849,
but was forced to obtain her advanced training abroad. In
1850 and 1852, however, special schools for medical training
for women were started in Philadelphia and Boston. By 1891
there were 1,300 women in medical training, compared with
over 18,000 men.

Progress in law was equally slow or slower: In 1900 there
were 151 women law students and 12,365 men. In graduate

schools proper, the story was somewhat better—
approximately 40 percent of graduate students in 1900
were women. Only in teaching and nursing did a significant
differential in admission rates favor women. In teaching, this
rate was apparently the result of the heavy male Civil War
casualties, which necessitated attracting women to fill open
positions.[7] The teacher training institutions were seminaries
and normal schools. By 1900 there were twice as many women
as men in teacher preparation. Initially, nursing schools almost uniformly had been attached to hospitals and as such
represented a somewhat different educational experience
from that prevailing in other fields, but from the beginning
nursing was predominantly a woman's profession.

Women in politics

Political activity was a second important area for women and
one in which they participated vigorously, sometimes on their
own behalf and sometimes on behalf of others. The suffrage
movement is usually dated from 1848, when a group of
women who had become acquainted with one another in
anti-slavery campaigns held a meeting. The meeting was con-
ceived at the Friend's Yearly Meeting, a rather logical development because the Quakers had always recognized the
equal rights of women. Lucretia Mott, Elizabeth Cady Stanton, Lucy Stone, Carrie Chapman Catt and Susan B. Anthony
were all leaders in the movement. The fight was long and slow
and gradual, progressing sporadically as the individual states,
one by one, enfranchised women. Finally, in 1919 a Constitu-
tional amendment, which stated that "the right to vote... shall
not be denied or abridged... on account of sex," passed both
Houses of Congress and was ratified by the required number
of states in 1920 to become the 19th Amendment.

Meanwhile, in a few isolated areas other legal gains had
been made. Oregon granted land to single and married
women in 1850, a concession that has been attributed to the

scarcity of women on the frontier and their consequent high
status. In general, however, the nineteenth century saw few
changes in the legal position of women.[8]

In many instances, women were involved in activities which
had a public-spirited motivation. High moral purpose was a
characteristic of the nineteenth century, and in the United
States, which believed deeply in progress and the march of
civilization, the role of social reformer was often taken by
women, who were considered the more "civilized" sex and
who also had less at stake in the business world. The relation
of this aim to education is eloquently expressed in the will of
Sophia Smith who, in leaving money for the founding of
Smith College, stated her hope that through education for
women "what are called their 'wrongs' will be redressed, their
wages adjusted, their weight of influence in reforming evils of
society will be greatly increased as teachers, as writers, as
mothers, as members of society, their power for good will be
incalculably enlarged."[9] Although their number was not
great, women leaders had emerged by the end of the
nineteenth century in a number of fields: Dorothea Dix in
hospital reform, Jane Addams in settlement house work,
Clara Barton and Lillian D. Wald in nursing, Ida R. Tarbell in
journalism, Charlotte Perkins Gilman in sociology, Frances
Willard in temperance work, Harriet Beecher Stowe and
Emily Dickinson in literature, M. Carey Thomas in education,
and Mary Baker Eddy in religion.

Just as the suffrage movement was in one sense an outgrowth of anti-slavery concerns, similarly, the temperance
movement, the movement to establish public parks, the wave
of concern about prostitution, and the struggle against child
labor all found women highly active and often militant. It is of
interest that in a list of 300 notable Americans compiled in
1953 by Richard B. Morris, a Columbia Professor of History,
and grouped by category, the only category in which women
outnumbered men was that of "Social Reform and Labor
Leader."[10]

The march of industrialization provided jobs that could be performed by women as well as, if not better than, men. Its rapid growth created a need for labor which was partly met by the employment of women and children. From the employer's standpoint such labor had the added advantage that it could be hired at a lower wage scale than adult male labor. Perhaps as a consequence, women were involved early in labor movements to improve working conditions. In the first half of the century Sarah Bagley, a mill worker, attempted with some success to organize women on a large scale Progress was slow, however, until the end of the century, when the International Ladies Garment Workers Union organized women on a large scale. In the early part of the twentieth century, inspired by the work of Emmeline Pankhurst, a British labor reformer, the trade union movement was joined with the suffrage movement and together mounted a series of effective strikes. These strikes, however, were seen more as a worker's struggle than a woman's issue, and women workers continued to receive lower pay than men.[11]

Female sexuality

Concurrently broader social changes were taking place that increased the freedom of women. These affected fashions in dress, attitudes toward sexual behavior, and customs in regard to independence. The prevailing attitudes toward women's sexuality were determined by nineteenth century Victorian beliefs which characterized women of the upper and middle classes (those to be emulated) as having no interest in, or enjoyment of, sexuality. Only lower-class women (i.e., depraved women or prostitutes) were thought to engage in sex with anything but distaste or as a marital duty.[12] This belief was based on the supposed "civilizing" impact of society, and in a sense was related to Darwin's theory of evolution. The process of evolution was confused with social advancement, so that those in the lower classes were felt to be closest to animals—that is, they had not evolved as far as the upper classes and therefore had more of an "animalistic" nature. How this accounted for the sexual proclivities of men is not clear, but presumably upper-class women were the most "civilized" of humans, and hence showed the least interest in sex.

These concepts about female sexuality began to break down under more objective medical observation, and particularly under the impact of Freud's discoveries and the writings of Havelock Ellis. Although currently Freud is a rather consistent target of attack by feminists, he was in large measure responsible for recognition in the world of science of the importance of sexual pleasure for women. Indeed, his initial descriptions of psychiatric illness in women related their illness to the lack of appropriate outlets for sexual impulses.[13] Hysteria, a common illness in women of his day, was found to be related to repressed sexual impulses and was cured by "lifting the repression." Furthermore, Freud took his women patients seriously. His writings and those of his followers had a tremendous influence on attitudes toward women's sexuality for the next seventy years.

Postwar changes

Although the first decade of the century saw some relaxation of Victorian attitudes, World War I greatly quickened the tempo of change. Thus, the 1920's saw a further social liberation and a considerable shift in sexual attitudes, which again influenced the position of women. Participation of women in athletics, the opening up of new job areas, changes in dress, acceptance of public smoking and drinking by women—all combined to shatter the Victorian image of the woman as a frail flower that must be protected. Parenthetically, it should be noted that this image of women had always been reserved for upper or middle-class women and was somehow preserved while at the same time lower-class women were considered capable of working long hours at arduous tasks, whether in factories or in domestic service.

In 1916 Margaret Sanger opened her first birth control clinic, and although she was jailed for it, she continued the fight to allow conception control.[14] Judge Ben Lindsey in COMPANIONATE MARRIAGE[15] and Bertrand Russell in MARRIAGE AND MORALS[16] suggested far-reaching innovations in social arrangements that would affect such previously sacred matters as marriage and the family or forbidden activities such as premarital sexual relationships. Although these views were not generally accepted, their appearance in the press is an indicator of the great change that had occurred to make possible the discussion of subjects previously taboo in "polite" society. Dress in this period underwent conspicuous change, with greatly shortened skirts, reduction in number of undergarments, and drastically new hair styles. The physical mobility of women was increased, while the automobile increased the geographic mobility of both sexes. Moreover, the automobile influenced social patterns of male-female relationships by providing easy access to complete privacy.

The Great Depression

The 1920's were followed by the Great Depression of the 1930's during which women of all classes were forced to help earn money outside the home, often because they could find jobs when men could not. This gave them a further taste of independence. It is probable, however, that this independence was not viewed positively at the time, occasioned as it was by economic necessity. This period also saw great advances in the development of labor-saving devices that made housekeeping something less than a full-time job when children were not involved. Women for the first time began to take an active part in the formal political structure. Several women were elected to Congress, one or two women became

Governors, and in 1933 Frances Perkins became the first woman appointed to the U. S. Cabinet.[17] Although the changes in sexual mores were not as dramatic, the trend started in the 1920's continued. Late in the 1930's improved contraceptives and the discovery of sulfa drugs reduced the prevailing fears of pregnancy and venereal disease.

World War II

World War II encompassed a second period of national disruption, with larger numbers of women than ever accepting jobs outside the home. Suddenly women found in the urgency of war production a great demand for their services, and all sorts of accommodations, such as day care facilities, were worked out to release them from home duties and child care. The period after World War II saw a vast explosion of technological advances. Almost everyone in the middle class could now own the major automatic home appliances that took so little time to operate. Developments in the food industry multiplied the number of convenience foods and further reduced the time required to run a home. "TV dinners" reached the status of a national joke. No longer were the roles of wife and mother the long-term full-time commitment they had been. Constraints on women to remain at home decreased. At the same time, many women who had elected these roles found they gave little satisfaction. Eventually all this led to a reconsideration of their assignment to women as primary occupations.

Furthermore, the medical advances of the earlier part of the century began to have far-reaching social effects. There was some increase in longevity, particularly for women, and a decrease in infant mortality. Improved methods of family planning and the high cost of raising children had effected a reduction in the number of children per family, at least in the middle and upper classes, during the Depression years. Although there was a great increase in the birthrate following

World War II, the means were available to limit family size and permit spacing of children, while the improved rates of infant survival decreased the number of pregnancies necessary to reach desired family size. Perhaps the single most important factor giving women control over their lives was the development of safe, relatively effective methods of contraception which could be used at the discretion of the woman. For the first time, a woman might have completed her family by age 24 or younger and be finished with the most demanding years of child-rearing by 40. This left approximately 30 years of predictable life without children to care for and meant that days were less than full unless other activities were found.[18]

Balanced against the decrease of necessary time spent in housekeeping was the widespread acceptance of Freud's dictum that the availability of the mother in early childhood is crucial for later healthy personality development. Freud concluded that maternal deprivation is one of the cardinal causes for later emotional difficulties. Many of Freud's case histories dwelt on improper child care by the nursemaids who served the middle-class families from which the majority of his patients were drawn. The implication was clear that inadequate "mothering" caused severe psychological disturbance. Later psychoanalytic writing recognized the importance of the child's ability to separate, but this concept received less popular attention.

These Freudian concepts were particularly prevalent between the two World Wars. As a result, women of the generation that came of age in the 1940's were determined to avoid what they felt were the mistakes of their parents by providing consistent, loving, available mothering to their children. This view was later buttressed by the work of Spitz and Cobliner[19] and Bowlby,[20] who presented the image of the institutionalized child, stunted in growth emotionally, intellectually and physically. This picture came to haunt middle-class parents whenever they were apart from their children, because these findings were interpreted to mean that women should stay at home, a conclusion probably further reinforced by the search for security after the disruptions of the Depression and World War II.

During the period between the two World Wars, in the realm of education there had been a gradual balancing of the numbers of men and women entering college. Equalization was somewhat delayed by the Depression, for a family that could afford to send only one child to college would, given the choice, tend to pick the male. By the time the United States had recovered from World War II, however, college for women, at least of the middle class, was a much more routine expectation, and, as the emphasis on credentials escalated, a B.A. became almost a necessity for the more interesting jobs. Nevertheless, the expectations of college continued to be different for women than for men, and college was not automatically thought to be preparation for a career. Thus, the entrance of women into the professions continued to lag. The numbers of women in law and medicine remained small and did not significantly increase until the mid-1960's.[21]

The beginning date for the "new" feminist movement of the past decade is variously ascribed. Some cite Simone de Beauvoir's THE SECOND SEX, published in 1953 in the U.S.A. (in 1949 in France), as the initiation point.[22] Alice Rossi, however, feels that de Beauvoir's book really signals the end of the preceding phase. Rossi considers the appointment and report of President Kennedy's Commission on the Status of Women in 1963 as the more significant event.[23] Others point to the Civil Rights movement, which to them suggests the parallel of women as another "oppressed" class. The lessons learned from the Civil Rights demonstrations were seen as a means to effect change in attitudes toward women much as they had toward Blacks. Betty Friedan's THE FEMININE MYSTIQUE published in 1963 was for many the opening salvo in the battle.[24] This was followed in 1966 by the formation of the National Organization for Women, which gave a structure to the strivings of individual women. An influential issue of *Daedulus* (1964) entitled "The Woman in America,"[25] provided important intellectual content, and SEXUAL POLITICS by Kate Millett, published in 1970, also received widespread attention.[26]

These several currents had flowed together by the late 1960's, when a full-blown feminist movement became evident. Other demographic factors contributed: For example, the mid-1960's saw the maturation of the first generation born after World War II. These young adults questioned, and often rejected, many of the more traditional patterns of life, including that of the nuclear family, accepted sexual patterns, and sex role stereotypes. The much-heralded sexual revolution may be more evolution than revolution, but it certainly insured continuing recognition and appreciation of the sexuality of women. The highly publicized work of Masters and Johnson was often interpreted to mean that women have a greater interest in, and potential for, sex than men. This represented an almost complete about-face from views held a century before.[27] Advances in contraceptive techniques gave women relatively easy ways to control conception, and antibiotics eliminated (or were supposed to have eliminated) the danger of venereal infections, thus minimizing the two long-standing practical deterrents to sexual intercourse. Dress styles became more informal for both men and women, eventually leading to the so-called "unisex" style. This detail in itself is perhaps unimportant, but it can be considered an example of the trend to deny differences between the sexes—at least differences that have any practical significance in terms of life style or possible behavior.

The sudden realization during this period that population control is a worldwide concern focused attention on the virtues of contraception and counteracted some of the traditional societal pressure to "propagate the race." Meanwhile, the continuing development of household machines and convenience foods further reduced the skills required to keep house, at the same time limiting the potential for a sense of satisfaction in the fulfillment of housekeeping respon- sibilities. Even the concept of the importance to the child of the availability of the mother at all times was challenged as too narrow an interpretation of Freud's concept, and many women began to realize that they did not necessarily want or need to devote the majority of their energies to their children, nor did the children need this exclusive devotion. On the political front, the passage by Congress of the Equal Rights Amendment in 1972 stressed further the general trend to- ward eliminating discrimination.

The Women's Movement

The Women's Movement is, of course, in no sense monolithic. It comprises a variety of groups, some of which have at least superficially conflicting goals. Nevertheless they are all in agreement that women should have equal rights with men and should resist accepting a state subservient to men. Some have interpreted this to mean that women should be totally "independent" of men, and as applied to the sexual sphere, this independence may mean supporting the lesbian position. Others see women's independence to mean the right openly to approach men, to enjoy relationships with them, and to end such relationships on the same basis that men have ended them in the past. All agree, however, that inequalities in pay and opportunities for advancement in work situations should be eliminated. Finally, many feel that affirmative action should be taken to correct imbalances resulting from past inequities.

The Women's Movement has stressed the right of women to control certain aspects of bodily function through contracep- tion and abortion, prohibitions against which are felt to have been enacted into law by men, who do not have to suffer the consequences of these laws. With great clarity and poignancy, women in and out of "the Movement" have specified a number of conditions which they find repugnant, unjust and discriminatory. For example, they define the state of women of all classes as one which predisposes women to failure in achieving personal fulfillment while imposing on them the frustrations of mundane housekeeping chores. They point to a system of sexual mores and marital arrangements that exploits and demeans their sexuality, citing the wife who feels she must trade sexual favors in return for her husband's financial support as a compelling illustration of this system. They feel that too often women must gratify their interests, needs and aspirations through those of their husbands and their children, and that women have come increasingly to assume vicarious identities, with the result that their personal self-expression has been stifled.

Thus, the decade of the 70's was ushered in by a feminist thrust toward goals in several different areas, involving a rather large number of women and enjoying widespread media coverage. Opposed to this trend was another group of women who take a more traditional view of women's roles and who saw the new feminism as somehow threatening. It is not entirely clear whether the threat was felt as a personal one or whether these women simply wished to dissociate themselves publicly from the feminist group, whose spokesmen frequently stated their opinions in the form of imperatives like "Women demand [this and that]," implying that all women agree with the particular demand. Despite this opposition, a widespread raising of consciousness has been felt well beyond the immediate reaches of feminist activities. Many women who do not look upon themselves as feminists are becoming increasingly aware of and increasingly vocal about social roles, attitudes and relationships which they begin to perceive as condescending, depreciating or overtly discriminatory, and which reinforce the traditional social structure in subtle ways. This awareness is perhaps keenest among young women in professional, academic, artistic and intellectual life. But already discussions about the kind of relationships they have with their boyfriends or husbands have begun to reach non-college women and to spill over into the popular magazines and onto the "chat" columns of the daily newspapers.

REFERENCES

1. Alice S. Rossi. "Equality between the Sexes: An Immodest Proposal," in THE WOMAN IN AMERICA, Robert J. Lifton, Ed. (Boston: Beacon Press, 1967) pp 98-143.
2. John Demos. "Myth and Reality in the History of American Family Life," in MARRIAGE PROBLEMS AND PROSPECTS, Henry Grunebaum & Jacob Christ, Eds. (Boston: Little, Brown, 1974).
3. Carl N. Degler. "Revolution without Ideology: The Changing Place of Women in America," in THE WOMAN IN AMERICA (Boston: Beacon Press, 1967) pp 193-210.
4. Demos, *op. cit.*
5. ENCYCLOPAEDIA BRITANNICA (Chicago: William Benton, 1963) Vol 23, pp 702 ff.
6. *Ibid.*
7. E. James Lieberman. American Families and the Vietnam War, *Journal of Marriage & the Family* 33 (1971): 709-722.
8. Degler, *op. cit.*
9. Thomas C. Mendenhall. The Report of the President, 1971-1972, *Smith College Bulletin* Series 67, No III (May 1973).
10. Richard B. Morris, Ed. ENCYCLOPEDIA OF AMERICAN HISTORY (New York: Harper & Brothers, 1953).
11. Connie Brown & Jane Seitz. "You've Come a Long Way, Baby: Historical Perspectives," in SISTERHOOD IS POWERFUL, Robin Morgan, Ed. (New York: Random House, 1970) pp 3-30.
12. William Acton. THE FUNCTIONS AND DISORDERS OF THE REPRODUCTIVE ORGANS (Philadelphia: Lindsay & Blakiston, 1867).
13. Sigmund Freud. "The Aetiology of Hysteria" (1896) in COLLECTED PAPERS (New York: Basic Books, 1960) Vol 1, Chapter 10, pp 183-219.
14. Margaret Sanger. AN AUTOBIOGRAPHY (New York: W. W. Norton, 1938).
15. Ben Lindsey. COMPANIONATE MARRIAGE (New York: Boni & Liveright, 1927).
16. Bertrand Russell. MARRIAGE AND MORALS (New York: Bantam Books, 1968).
17. Cynthia Fuchs Epstein. WOMAN'S PLACE (Berkeley, Calif.: University of California Press, 1971).

18. Rossi, *op. cit.*

19. Rene Spitz & W. Godfrey Cobliner. FIRST YEAR OF LIFE: A PSYCHOANALYTIC STUDY OF NORMAL AND DEVIANT DEVELOPMENT OF OBJECT RELATIONS (New York: International Universities Press, 1966).

20. John Bowlby. ATTACHMENT (New York: Basic Books, 1969).

21. Esther Peterson. "Working Women," in THE WOMAN IN AMERICA (Boston: Beacon Press, 1967) pp 144-172.

22. Simone DeBeauvoir. THE SECOND SEX (New York: Bantam Books, 1963).

23. President's Commission on the Status of Women. AMERICAN WOMEN: REPORT OF THE PRESIDENT'S COMMISSION (Washington, D.C.: Government Printing Office, 1963).

24. Betty Friedan. THE FEMININE MYSTIQUE (New York: Dell Publishing, 1963).

25. "The Woman in America," *Daedalus* 93, 2 (Spring 1964); also available as THE WOMAN IN AMERICA (Boston: Beacon Press, 1967).

26. Kate Millett. SEXUAL POLITICS (New York: Avon Books, 1971).

27. William H. Masters & Virginia E. Johnson. HUMAN SEXUAL RESPONSE (Boston: Little, Brown, 1966).

3

EXPECTATIONS OF WOMEN IN THE COLLEGE CONTEXT

The college or university, frequently if not always, mirrors the ambivalent attitudes of the general society toward women, and, despite stated goals to the contrary, at times inadvertently reinforces many of the existing female stereotypes. While higher education in America, as elsewhere, was originally for men only, women have made important inroads here, and the idea of equal education for women has become more and more accepted. At the present time over 40 percent of all college undergraduates are women. Women not only are encouraged to enter college, but are expected to compete successfully with men in academic pursuits and in actual fact their academic performance at college is often superior.

While American society has gone as far as any in providing higher education for women, it has not equally provided opportunities for women to make use of the education they have received. Those undergraduate women who plan to enter a career find that, while theoretically many are open to women, theory and practice do not always mesh. If one looks at the statistics of women college graduates, one finds that most of those employed have found placement in elementary school education, the nursing profession, and office and sales work. Women represent less than 1 percent of engineers, 2 percent of executives, and 7 percent of physicians. While these figures have begun to climb upward, there remains a paradox in the apparent encouragement of women in college.[1]

College women who might otherwise seek intellectual and professional development face other discouragements. One very visible negative message is conveyed to them by the small percentage of female faculty members they see in college. With the exception of women's colleges, women faculty are in a small minority, and even at some women's colleges the balance is shifting toward men. In 1972-73 there was one woman for every ten men who were full professors in American colleges, and even this ratio was improved by the inclusion of 2-year colleges. At the more prestigious universities only a handful, something like 2 percent of the full professors, 4 or 5 percent of the associate professors, and 10 percent of the assistant professors were women.[2] These ratios convey to women students a sense of limited access. Given the importance of models for intellectual and occupational development, they also deny women students sources of identification and advice that are available to their male colleagues.

Women's aspirations are also discouraged by attitudes of male faculty and male fellow students, who intimate (and sometimes openly state) that women's primary place is in the home to the exclusion of a career. Often it is implied that women should seek a "suitable" job as an interim occupation before they assume their ultimate role as wife, homemaker and mother. Sometimes this interim occupation is expected to help support a husband through his graduate school years. It is not unusual for a college woman whose aspirations do not follow this pattern to be asked by her faculty adviser—usually male—"Why does a pretty girl like you want to attend law school?" The implication here is clear: A "normal" female student chooses marriage as her goal. In this stereotyped view women only plan serious careers when they are either somewhat "odd" or not pretty enough to attract an offer of marriage. Despite the Women's Liberation movement, the traditional view that women's proper role is that of wife and mother is still widely held by parents, employers, and even educators. It is also held by many young women themselves.

The implicit assumption prevails that this role was ordained by nature and has persisted unchanged through the ages.

Although it is implied that the "norm" is for a woman to become exclusively a wife and mother, current statistics indicate that 50 percent of women in the United States hold a job outside the home; this includes almost one-third of all mothers of preschool children. The higher the educational attainment of a woman, the greater the likelihood that she will work outside the home. More than half of all women college graduates are employed, 71 percent of all women with some postgraduate education[3] and 91 percent of women doctorate holders, almost all on a full-time basis.[4] It is clear, however that many work at job levels lower than their educational attainments would suggest were appropriate. While most women work for economic reasons, participation in the labor force is by no means restricted to low-income groups. In 1971, 41 percent of the families in the top 5 percent income bracket had working wives.[5]

Along with negative attitudes toward women pursuing careers, aspersions on the intellectual capacities of women are frequently reported by women students. Although there are signs that these attitudes are diminishing among male undergraduates, many male students persist in the notion that women do not possess the same objective rationality as men. Studies by investigators show a persistent tendency by many, though by no means all women, to "play dumb" in the presence of men so as to conform to the stereotype. Other studies have shown that women's career aspirations are heavily influenced by the attitudes of the male whom they are dating or otherwise close to. Furthermore, it is frequently distressing for the college woman to find that her "enlightened" male fellow student believes in sexual equality and the right of women to pursue their own careers—until it affects him directly. Case vignette 2 illustrates the point:

> Nancy had an outstanding academic record in her major of biology. She had considered applying to medical school

but decided that she would prefer to teach biology either at college or secondary school. To this end she was encouraged to apply for graduate school by her faculty adviser and was accepted at a prominent Midwestern university.

In her senior year Nancy had become involved with Ben, a fellow senior, who was pre-Med. They met initially in a biology class and he seemed very admiring of her intellectual abilities. Their relationship developed and both thought in terms of marriage, although they made no definite decision. Ben was accepted at an Eastern medical school which was his first choice. He was also accepted at a midwestern school within commuting distance of the university by which Nancy was accepted. With very little hesitation he chose the Eastern School.

The ensuing discussion brought out clearly Ben's view that he was quite amenable to Nancy working and even having "a career" but that his career was really the crucial one. Consequently, he had no intention of modifying his decision because of Nancy. Nancy was so upset by Ben's attitude and his apparent inflexibility when put to the test that their relationship cooled considerably, and by graduation it was not clear whether they would continue to see each other.

Outside of the strictly academic sphere, the campus culture often assigns a restricted role to women. In coeducational institutions, women rarely hold major positions in student government, newspapers, or athletics. In 1970 women constituted only 5 percent of student-body presidents, 12 percent of judicial board chairmen, and 25 percent of newspaper editors.[6] By contrast their role as sex objects is highlighted in such ceremonies as that of Homecoming Queen. Although several colleges have recently abolished this particular ritual, there are students, both male and female, who feel it should be continued.

Until a few years ago much of campus life and the regulations governing it were concerned with the "protection" of women, which usually meant preserving their chastity. Elaborate parietal rules, while ostensibly guarding "morality," indirectly stressed that women were to be thought of in a primarily sexual role.[7] The woman's overprotected and restricted life thus limited opportunities for her to develop a healthy autonomy. In contrast, men on campus have always had greater freedom and many more options which better serve the possibility of their autonomous growth. The virtual elimination of parietal rules in many colleges across the nation is one indicator that changes are taking place in the attitudes toward, and the situation of, women. Women are beginning to be perceived as capable of making their own decisions about relationships and of implementing these decisions once they have made them. But there is still a considerable way to go.

In other respects, colleges have been neglectful of the fact that nearly half of their students are women. Courses in history, sociology, and psychology have neglected the contributions women have made to culture, a neglect that women's studies programs are now remedying in part. College services have failed to provide the support services that women especially need—for example, information and counseling on birth control, pregnancy and abortion. To this day such vital services as those of a gynecologist may be either not available at all or not readily available. Such services may not be offered in the student health program on campus, or they may be offered only at an additional charge when other medical care is covered by the general health fee. Advisory services that would specifically orient women toward graduate and professional schools and toward careers have been distinguished either by their absence or by the weakness of their support. Recommendations written for women students applying for jobs or graduate study often feature such qualities as "attractiveness" and "femininity," which are not relevant to the ability to study or to perform on a job.

Many other practices of collegiate institutions have worked to the particular detriment of women. Admissions procedures often have been discriminatory. Some institutions have set higher criteria of admission for women than they have for men, creating an imbalance that is detrimental to both sexes. Some coeducational institutions admit a smaller percentage of women than of men. The origin of this last-named practice is not entirely clear, but it seems to be related to the social philosophy that having more men than women in a social situation represents a social mix more advantageous to the woman, perhaps not unlike those formal dances at which a surplus of men (stagline) is provided so that none of the girls need be wallflowers. This practice has reinforced the definition of women as sex objects and has inhibited the process of acquaintance out of which more mature heterosexual relations can develop.

In addition, there are difficulties of reentry to an educational institution and of transfer from one institution to another including problems concerning transfer of credits. For married women, this has created difficulties because, if their choice of school is determined by their husbands, as it often is, they need to be able to move between institutions without loss of credit. Social customs which dictate that wives should follow their husbands reinforce these difficulties and frequently place the woman in the uncomfortable position of apparently having to choose between marriage and career.

The treatment of women highlights the general tendency of our educational institutions to shape higher education in relation to the needs of men but not women. We tend to conceive of preparation for a career as a process which progresses continuously and we are suspicious of interruptions. Some Ph.D. programs set a limited time period for obtaining the degree which particularly disadvantages those, usually women, who may wish to study less than full time. More help is needed for women who, after completing college, wish to pursue a career but are also faced with household demands. For women who, while their children are young, plan to spend the years primarily in the home, continuation of career training or some practice in a career is currently very difficult to arrange. There is a lack of high-level part-time professional jobs, and, after taking time off to start a family, many women find reentry into the career mainstream very difficult.

Furthermore, educational institutions have failed to meet the challenge of helping women maintain some level of intellectual activity during the peak period of family care. Many women in the "diaper years" have felt a sense of depletion and anxiety about the atrophy of their intellectual abilities which they would not need to experience if our educational system recognized this problem and took such steps toward its solution as providing part-time educational programs or jobs. Finally, few institutions make more than a minimal attempt to offer opportunities to women who wish seriously to pursue further education in their middle years.

Against this campus background, what are the expectations of today's college women? Sometimes they are confused or at best unclear, as the following statements written to gain admission at one college to a course on "The Educated Woman" would indicate:

> STATEMENT #2: Although I've had no formal experience with the study of women, my interest in this seminar is primarily a personal one; because I intend to continue with education, I'll most likely qualify some day as an "educated woman." At present, I have no specific career or "future" plans and would approach this study in light of my own, and my female peers', futures.

> STATEMENT #3: My little thinking about my role as an educated woman before I came to college never had a real testing ground, for I had always lived largely apart from men in my family of 6 girls and my two schools for girls. When I came to college I was struck by some realization about this role I had (the need to do something because I was a woman, etc.). The novelty of a coed environment and its implications socially and academically have changed my thinking, made it more realistic, more exciting, but often more discouraged.

STATEMENT #4: I sense many conflicts within myself as to what constitutes a definition of an "educated woman." I read in a recent issue of a new magazine *Ms* about a study conducted at the University of Michigan which showed that women have a greater tendency not to succeed, the higher they pursue their education. Why is this? Does an "educated woman" have to be a super-woman who can reconcile career and family goals so well that neither suffers at the expense of the other? Unfortunately my background in this whole area is very weak, which is why I would like to be in this seminar.

Expectations depend in part on personal background and experience, and in part on the cultural setting in which a woman finds herself, but there are discernible changes at work. Recent surveys of entering college freshmen conducted by the American Council on Education show that, while most college women continue to view marriage and the raising of a family as important personal goals, a steadily increasing number expect to combine family with career commitments.[8] Women are planning to marry later and to have smaller families than they planned even five years ago. Many are beginning to realize that, as a consequence of their desire for smaller families, the availability of contraception and abortion, and today's longer life-span, they will be devoting a relatively small portion of their adult lives to child-rearing. Many are also influenced by those contemporary attitudes which reject the assignment of roles or status on the basis of race, socioeconomic background, or sex, and which put a premium on individualism and autonomy.

In the past, many women who pursued careers remained single or came to a career after their husbands died. Career women who married and raised a family were able to do so because they could find and afford adequate domestic help. Today's young women face a different situation. Domestic help is difficult if not impossible to find, and child care centers are scarce. The graduated income tax means that the second

wage earner (usually the wife) must earn at a relatively high
rate just to break even. Thus, practical problems for married
working women remain serious today even though they differ
from problems of the past, and few women have adequate
models after whom they can pattern their own lives as they try
to cope with newly evolving styles of family life.

Over and above the practical problems for women seeking a
career, there may be internal barriers built up in the course of
growing up. Differences in the way boys and girls are
socialized are well known. In a recent paper, Jeanne Block has
aptly described the effects of some of them:

> For males, socialization tends to enhance experiential op-
> tions and to encourage more androgynous sex role defini-
> tions since some traditionally feminine concerns (conscien-
> tiousness, conservation, interdependency) are emphasized
> along with the press to renounce negative aspects of
> the masculine role: opportunism, restlessness, self-
> centeredness. For women, the socialization process tends to
> reinforce the nurturant, docile, submissive, and conserva-
> tive aspects of the traditionally defined female role and
> discourages personal qualities conventionally defined as
> masculine: self-assertiveness, achievement orientation, and
> independence. The sex role definitions and behavioral op-
> tions for women, then, are narrowed by the socialization
> process, whereas, for men, the sex-role definitions are
> broadened by socialization. The achievement of higher
> levels of ego functioning for women is more difficult be-
> cause individuation involves conflict with our prevailing
> cultural norms.[9]

Thus, women are prepared for the traditional role of wife and
mother and internal barriers are created which militate
against a "career" as opposed to "work," interim or indefinite
in term. These barriers can be seen to arise from a variety of
factors, both conscious and unconscious, and although it is
clearly impossible to draw a sharp line between the conscious

and the unconscious, it may be helpful to start with these categories in mind.

Two major contributing influences are one's expectations of oneself and one's apperception of the expectations of others as they apply to oneself or perhaps to a group with which one is identified such as "college women." These expectations, conscious and unconscious, are often related to each other. Thus, one woman may consciously expect herself to use her talents to their fullest, but unconsciously she may devalue those talents to such a degree that she perceives a serious career as impossible. Similarly with regard to the expectations of others—for example, she may consciously feel that her parents have no particular expectation of how she will arrange her life so that theoretically she could pursue a professional career without their disapproving. Unconsciously, however, she may recognize that her mother put a premium on full-time homemaking and in consequence she may fear that any other choice will be unacceptable in the eyes of her parents.

These concepts lead to a more general consideration of the girl's identity formation and her eventual self-image. One important facet of her identity will be her conception of what it means to be a woman. This conception will be influenced by familial values, societal attitudes and personal experiences, all interacting with the physical and psychological attributes with which the individual is endowed at birth. Once developed, the self-image interacts with the girl's vision of what qualities are required to follow a particular life path successfully and what the implications are if she does. Thus, if a girl feels that to be successful in business one must be sharp, aggressive, and willing to sacrifice one's "personal" life, this feeling may clash with her sense of her abilities and inclinations, or, more complexly, with her concept of the behavior "appropriate" to a woman.

Similar considerations can obviously affect the boy's choice of a career, but, as Block points out, his vision of what is

required of him to be a business success is much more likely to
be consonant with the traditional stereotype of male traits and
the male role.[10] The woman, however, feels faced with the
dilemma of either abandoning the idea of the career or changing radically her self concept, which may be very difficult to do
and may not seem worth doing.

A logical extension of this problem is the woman's view of
her relationship to men and how it may be affected by her
choice of career. This may be complicated by more than
internal factors if she is actually involved with a man not
willing to be flexible in regard to her career plans, and the relationship ends. Should the experience be repeated, the young
woman will inevitably begin to ponder the difficulties that
career choice has created for her personal life. If there is any
uncertainty in her mind (and in what college student is there
not uncertainty?) she may wonder whether the end is worth
the losses along the way. It may require considerable faith or
courage to forge ahead, either trusting that eventually a relationship with a man can be worked out or risking not having
such a relationship.

One could say that the man is in a similar position, but two
societal attitudes make for a critical difference: first, the view
still generally prevailing (and actually the legal fact) that a
man is responsible for providing his family's support—thus,
embarking on a career is seen as an approved and even necessary preparatory step for establishing a permanent relationship with a woman; second, the corollary view that the woman
does not need to earn a living because the man will provide for
her—thus, she may be seen as deliberately complicating her
life by even considering a career.

In the area of intelligence many stereotyped and frequently
inaccurate ideas have been accepted unquestioningly by many
young women and by many of their male peers, who feel that
intelligence and logical thinking are "biologically" masculine
attributes and that a woman therefore enters with a built-in
handicap any field in which these attributes are important.

Or, where a young woman is aware that her own intelligence is equivalent to that of the men with whom she has been associated, either in school or socially, she may nevertheless worry that showing her intelligence will affect her relationships with men. Although neither attitude may be clearly perceived by the woman on a conscious level, both feelings may join to create a very real internal obstacle to her choice of a serious career. Or because she accepts the societal view that the wife should not outperform the husband, the women student may conclude that professional success will reduce the available pool of eligible men for her to choose from.

Closely related to a male-female relationship is the issue of motherhood and child-rearing, for the ability to have children is closely related to the concept of being a woman. Quite apart from the practicalities of caring for children, most girls will have some anticipatory view of themselves as mothers. This view will probably be most deeply influenced by the girl's own childhood experience or by her distorted memories of this experience. It may also be affected by popular attitudes toward child-rearing, particularly attitudes prevalent in the peer culture and attitudes expressed by potential husbands. If the girl herself has some feeling that motherhood should be a full-time occupation at least during the child's preschool years, this feeling may turn her away from any career that is seen as requiring consistent endeavor if it is to be rewarding or successful. Conversely, she may feel that commitment to a career at a time when motherhood is not a real possibility will only cause severe conflict in the event she does marry and the option to have a child is thrown open to her. In short, she may fear that the difficulties of combining a career with marriage and family are so great that one of them must be sacrificed. Rather than make the choice of career while in college and find out when the time comes whether marriage and children cannot be integrated with it, she will choose marriage and family and, if they are not immediately attainable, occupy herself with an interim job. The following comment by a woman with a graduate degree, made in answer to the question in a survey of women with advanced degrees, "Do you feel that you confronted special problems in employment or education because you are a woman?" illustrates several of these points.

> STATEMENT #5: I have never encountered any discrimination on account of sex, unless possibly favorable discrimination. The special problems I have had come not from being a woman, but from being a married woman. I have had to change jobs twice because of moves my husband made, one of which was necessary and one clearly beneficial to him. This is a problem both partners would be likely to have to face in any marriage in which both are committed to careers. In both job changes, I found a position suitable to my qualifications; both my husband and I held out for that. Both changes were probably, on balance, good for me. Nevertheless, this is a special problem that someone who is not married, or someone whose career is clearly identified as the dominant one (in our society, usually still the husband's), need not face.
>
> The other two problems I have had to deal with have come from being a woman who decided to have children as well as a career. The practical as well as the emotional strain of implementing that decision is great. Pregnancy and recovery create a problem with regard to work that, however it is solved, is obviously a problem no man has to deal with. Once the existence of children is taken care of, one's life (and one's husband's) depends upon the quality of child care available. These are not exactly problems in employment, but they are closely connected with employment; either they affect work, or work affects them.
>
> Needless to say, if I had married before finishing my education, that, too, might have been influenced. As it was, my commitment to my studies probably influenced me to marry later than many girls in our society.

Another influence that may affect a woman's internal motivation is the current reality of the difficulties for women in many fields. This realistic situation may prompt a kind of depressive or apathetic response—it's not worth the fight, or, why try when even men are having trouble getting jobs? For the man to take such a position is not so easy because of society's expectations of him and its pressure on him to pursue a career so that he will be able to support a family. (Recently, however, the phenomenon of "dropping out" of society by some men may incorporate some of these elements.) For the woman, however, there is an alternative that is not only acceptable but that also promises certain satisfactions (whether they materialize or not) in the form of companionship, motherhood and financial support. Of course, there are always a few women who react oppositely, women who, if told that a given field is virtually closed to them, will consider this a challenge and deliberately enter it. In general, however, this reaction is more atypical for women than for men and acting it out may be blocked by the woman's concept of what is "appropriate" behavior for a woman.

In the long run everyone, male and female, will attempt to chart a life course calculated to bring maximum gratification to the best of the individual's ability to predict. This ability, however, may be severely limited by early experiences, unconscious identifications, and complex expectations. Rarely will these all mesh and point unequivocally in one direction; more often they will in some measure conflict, so that a satisfactory resolution becomes difficult or impossible. When reconciliation of conflicting feelings is not possible, a choice must be made and it is at this point that external factors can enter to act as a determining factor by supporting or canceling out one or another of the contradictory internal elements. Thus, it is probably impossible to limit discussion to internal obstacles, because it is the complex interplay of internal feelings with external realities that is in the end crucial to the individual woman's choice. The following answer to a question about career difficulties illustrates this interplay:

> STATEMENT #6: The worst problem I had to overcome was within myself, i.e., the feeling that I needn't be serious about

graduate school and a career because I was going to get married and be supported by my husband. Almost every female academic I know has faced or is facing this problem in some guise.

Putting aside this emotional problem, I faced very real discrimination when I went looking for a job (late 1968-early 1969). Several potential employers told me at our convention that they were looking for someone, but would not consider a woman, even though my credentials were excellent. When I took the job at [X university] I was hired as a Lecturer, even though I had my Ph.D., and in addition, I was paid less than three men also hired that year, none of whom had completed the doctorate.

The emphasis on career in the foregoing discussion is not meant to obscure the fact that for many women the job of wife and mother provides a complete and fulfilling life. The choice of career or combined marriage and career must not be set up as a standard against which all college women should measure themselves; these roles should be seen rather as alternatives. They have been stressed in contrast to the homemaker role because many influences in our culture today press women into the latter position.

REFERENCES

1. U. S. Bureau of the Census. OCCUPATION BY INDUSTRY (Washington, D.C.: Govt Ptg Ofc, 1970), No. PC-7C, 1970.
2. Women Today 3, 6 (Mar. 19, 1973).
3. U. S. Department of Labor, Wage and Standards Administration. Women's Bureau TRENDS IN EDUCATIONAL ATTAINMENT OF WOMEN (Washington, D. C.: Govt. Ptg. Ofc., 1967).
4. Helen W. Astin. THE WOMAN DOCTORATE IN AMERICA (New York: Russell Sage Foundation, 1969).
5. Wall Street Journal (Mar. 15, 1972) page 3.
6. Juanita Kreps. SEX IN THE MARKETPLACE: AMERICAN WOMEN AT WORK (Baltimore: The Johns Hopkins University Press, 1971).
7. Group for the Advancement of Psychiatry. SEX AND THE COLLEGE STUDENT, Report No. 60 (New York: GAP, 1965).

8. Alexander Astin *et al.* THE AMERICAN FRESHMAN: NATIONAL NORMS FOR FALL 1973. American Council of Education, University of California at Los Angeles (Washington, D.C.: The Council, 1974).

9. Jeanne H. Block. Conceptions of Sex Role: Some Cross-Cultural and Longitudinal Perspectives, *American Psychologist* 28 (1973): 512-527.

10. *Ibid.*

4

THE FEMININE-MASCULINE AXIS

Some of the problems facing college women have been discussed, while factors and concepts relating to woman's social role, her self concept and self-expectations have been cited as bearing significantly on these problems, as have society's view of, attitude toward, and expectations for women. There are biological, developmental and sociocultural factors that define the similarities and differences between men and women. These are important because such clichés as "It's a woman's nature" or "It's characteristically masculine" are used in explanation and justification of certain role assignments and certain characteristics of male-female relationships. The rationale for these views and their source need to be examined.

The crux of the issue involves a questioning and redefinition of the role of women in our society. The traditional view is that the male and female roles assigned are determined by "nature," which is defined to mean the differential biological and psychological characteristics of the male and the female. The new view is that many of these characteristics are in reality determined by social conditioning and those which are not so determined need not, in most instances, function as role determinants. The thrust of this new view is toward equality of opportunity for both sexes, the implication being that, if such equality were to be achieved, the sexes would be represented equally in most roles—suggesting that men and women are generally similar in their capabilities. This assumption has been questioned by those who believe that males and females constitutionally have bodies, emotional patterns, and interests which are characteristic of their sex and make them fit or unfit for certain tasks. Although there are research data to support both views, they are often cited in attack or defense of positions that may be espoused for specific political purposes or because of unconscious attitudes, rather than as objective judgments.

The terms *masculinity* and *femininity* sum up many of the facts known and many of the feelings people have about the sexes. A definition of these concepts becomes crucial in bringing some order to the confusion surrounding them, in clarifying the range of options for both sexes, and in outlining the limits, if any, as they apply to social roles. Furthermore, the definitions of these terms have an important bearing on the issue of self-fulfillment "as a woman" or "as a man." The question then arises, are there any specific experiences that a female or a male must have to achieve fulfillment or do these experiences differ for every individual, whether male or female, with the content of these experiences determined by learned values and not by sex? Although our knowledge is incomplete, it would seem important to examine what we do know about these matters if we are to ascertain how they affect the social roles of women and men. Clearly, they are not easy matters to sort out, but we will try to separate biological from cultural factors, and to identify where possible some of the psychological and social variables that affect concepts of male and female, masculine and feminine.

Definitions of sex and gender

One of the great problems in discussing men and women, their roles and relationships, is the confusion in terminology and the lack of precision characterizing its use. Terms like *male* and *female* or *masculine* and *feminine* are used loosely without specification as to whether one is referring to a biological attribute, cultural stereotype, physiological characteristic, or some second-order association of trait with sex—for example, the trait of aggressiveness with the male. One might assume that the terms *male* and *female* are quite clear, but recent research on anomalies in the newborn has underlined the difficulties in certain cases even in the assignment of sex, that is, determining whether an individual is male or female. Terms like *sexual identity* and *gender identity* are also used to describe without clear differentiation the individual's internal self-image as a male or female or the individual's preferred mode of sexual behavior as heterosexual or homosexual. Finally, the terms *sex role* and *gender role* seem to suggest a description of the individual's functioning in a social context as a male or a female, but given the fact that male and female roles differ greatly from culture to culture and even from group to group within a culture, it is difficult to ascertain the true meaning of the terms unless one also defines the social context.

Because these imprecise definitions are frequently used in ignorant and/or partisan fashion, and argument is secondarily based on their assigned meanings, it seems particularly important to define them in this report as clearly as possible and to adhere to these definitions throughout.

The dictionary is of relatively little help, but it does define *sex* as "one of the two divisions of...human beings respectively designated male or female."[1] John Money has pointed out, however, that even this division is not easily defined in a scientific sense.[2] He cites five biological factors that are involved: (1) Nuclear sex, as demonstrated by chromosome pattern; (2) gonadal sex, by the presence of testes or ovaries; (3) hormonal sex, by the pattern of hormonal productions; (4) internal accessory structures, by uterus or prostate; and (5) external genital morphology, by penis and testes or vagina. In most individuals all five factors are consonant, and assignment of sex is based on external genital morphology. Thus, when a baby is born, the genitals are inspected and the child is designated a girl or a boy on this basis. When external genital morphology is ambiguous, as it sometimes is, suggesting lack of consonance in the five factors, other factors must be considered, which is beyond the scope of this discussion. It has become quite clear, however, that *sex of assignment and rearing, that is, how the parents define and respond to the child's sex, are the most important influences in determining the individual's later internal sense of being male or female.*

Gender is defined by the dictionary mainly in reference to grammar, that is, those words which are of masculine or feminine gender in certain languages.[3] Money and Ehrhardt define *gender identity* and *gender role* as follows:

> **Gender identity:** The sameness, unity, and persistence of one's individuality as male, female, or ambivalent, in greater or lesser degree, especially as it is experienced in self-awareness and behavior; gender identity is the private experience of gender role, and gender role is the public expression of gender identity.

> **Gender role:** Everything that a person says and does, to indicate to others or to the self the degree that one is either male, or female, or ambivalent; it includes but is not restricted to sexual arousal and response; gender role is the public expression of gender identity, and gender identity is the private experience of gender role.[4]

Sexual orientation usually refers to the preferred adult sexual behavior of the individual as heterosexual, homosexual or bisexual, and will be so used in preference to the more ambiguous term, *sexual identity.*

Biological aspects of male and female

Generally speaking, most animal species are divided into two subclasses, males and females, each having characteristic anatomical features, patterns of physiological response, and specific ways of relating to each other. One way of relating which embraces all three sets of characteristics is sexual and is essential for reproduction. This holds true for human beings, who display all three characteristics but, in addition, may have certain culturally imposed differences, such as style of dress, mode of grooming, or life tasks also assigned on the basis of sex. The terms *masculine* and *feminine* are adjectives used to denote characteristics associated with either males or females. These characteristics may be based on biological, physiological, psychological, or behavioral attributes, some of which may be inherited and some learned, while many will result from the interaction between inheritance and learning.

One of the most noteworthy characteristics of the human species is the capacity for considerable plasticity, which is combined with the ability to adapt in many diverse ways. Among these is the ability to interchange almost totally under appropriate circumstances behavior generally assigned as masculine with that assigned as feminine. Such is the enormous capacity of the human psyche for adaptation that it seems as though almost the entire range of behavioral characteristics can be developed by a member of either sex. Furthermore, cross-cultural studies indicate that human cultures vary widely in those traits and activities specifically assigned as masculine or feminine. In fact, the same trait is often assigned the opposite sex by two different cultures.[5] For example, in many cultures, heavy physical work is assigned to women, whereas in our culture it is more often thought of as a male activity.

Male and female go through stages in their development both biologically and psychologically, so that their attributes change over time, as do characterizations of masculinity and femininity. A particularly important change biologically, physiologically and psychologically occurs at the time of puberty, when hormonal patterns alter, secondary sex characteristics appear, and both males and females become biologically ready for their respective reproductive roles. At this point the biological differences between males and females become more sharply marked, and certain patterns of sexual response are to be found in both males and females—for example, they react in arousal response to each other; however, some adults will display patterns of arousal to individuals of the same sex, indicating that other factors can intervene to prevent development of the usual response. Because sexual behavior is one sphere in which male and female play clearly different roles, it is not unnaturally related to concepts of masculinity and femininity.

Although the relationship of sexual behavior to masculinity and femininity is not likely to be disputed, even this connection has become remarkably complex as a result of increasing knowledge. Gadpaille, in an excellent review article, refers to the many variables which must be considered here, and he outlines areas of current knowledge as well as of ignorance.[6] His review undertakes to integrate a large amount of animal experimentation designed to isolate central nervous system and hormonal factors in sexual behavior, advances in the understanding of human sexual behavior through the study of various pathological human conditions involving chromosomal or hormonal anomalies, and more careful studies of developmental influences on gender identity. The correlations between these studies are complex and somewhat speculative, but a summary of Gadpaille's conclusions may be useful.

Experiments have determined that in rats there is a critical fetal period during which the presence of androgen (male hormone) will cause (1) the development of normal male genitalia, (2) the organization of the brain in such a way that a male pattern of hormonal release is established, and (3) the exhibiting in the adult rat of male sexual behavior in response to a female. The absence of androgen at the critical fetal period will result in female morphology, female hormonal release patterns, and female sex response behavior in *all* rats regardless of whether they are of male or female genotype (i.e., chromosomal pattern).

Studies on primates are less advanced but so far have tended to give similar results. In addition to influences during gestation, it has been observed that adult sexual behavior will not be displayed by primates unless the developing individuals have had adequate mothering, peer group social contact, and childhood sex play. This suggests the increasing importance of the cerebral cortex and of socialization processes to sexual behavior as one approaches the human level in the phylogenetic scale. Although research which requires laboratory intervention during the gestational process obviously cannot be conducted with human subjects, certain "natural" developmental anomalies have been observed which mimic some of those found in laboratory experimental conditions and bear out many of the findings from animal research.

Gadpaille draws several conclusions from these data. The first is that female morphology is basic, regardless of genotype, and males develop only when androgen is present in appropriate quantity during a critical fetal period. This androgen, when present, has two effects: (1) It governs the development of normal male morphology with regard to genitalia, and (2) it organizes a part of the brain in a particular (masculine) way so that it will later function with respect to hormonal output in the normal male (acyclic) manner. Without androgen, female genitalia will develop (although female genotype is necessary for procreative functioning) and the relevant part of the brain will be organized to release hormones in the female (cyclic) manner. Gadpaille believes that this part of the brain also affects later sexual response. He recognizes, however, that as species rise in the phylogenetic scale, socialization processes become more crucial in determining sexual outcome, and that as the human level is reached, rearing can dominate all other factors in deciding self concepts of gender identity and adult sexual response.

Gadpaille also cites a statistical study that distinguished males from females on a series of criteria including energy

level, toy and sports preferences, and basis for erotic arousal.
Although he recognizes the possibility that some of these
criteria may be culturally determined, he feels that others are
clearly independent of cultural influence, and he explains
these differences as arising from differences in brain organization caused by the presence or absence of androgen in the
critical fetal period. "It seems likely," he says, "that there are
definable differences in masculine and feminine behavior,
attitudes, and preferences that are traceable to the simple
biological fact of being male or female (assuming biologically
normal development) and that all such differences are not
purely cultural artifacts."[7] On the other hand, he recognizes
that, for any individual, sex of assignment and rearing
(whether the child is brought up as a boy or a girl) can out-
weigh all other factors.

It should be noted that other observers take issue with
Gadpaille's conclusions, but his thinking is an indication of
current research attempts to illuminate a controversial
subject.[8] Thus, although gender identity will almost always be
determined by sex of assignment and rearing, what deter-
mines gender role and adult sex response is more
problematic—as the controversy engendered by Gadpaille's
conclusions illustrates—but clearly it must be discussed in
considering the roles of women and men. Biological, environmental, sociological and moral issues continually and
variably complicate our psychological conceptualizations. In
understanding concepts of masculinity and femininity, should
our emphasis be upon the perceived differences or upon the
actual and anticipated similarities in function, personality,
and even appearance? The current strivings for sex equality
carry with them a certain tendency toward similarity between
the sexes, a single life style for both males and females, a
sameness of function except where anatomically unrealizable
in the most restricted sense. This point of view, and the real
proposals which accompany it, are based on assumptions that
(1) males and females are essentially the same and (2) where

they are not the same, emotionally and behaviorally, it is as the result of social learning, and social learning—theoretically, at least—is alterable, so that (3) the two sexes can be *made* more equal and similar.

Thus there are two opposing views in currency today: One view posits that there are indeed innate biophysiological differences between the sexes, some of which may be modified by social conditioning, but only through specific efforts to do so; the other view contends that almost all emotional and behavioral differences are a product of the socialization process. Proponents of the two views may also differ significantly on the benefits of minimizing the differences. Somewhere between these two propositions one finds the psychoanalytic view that the fact of the anatomical distinctiveness of each sex leads inevitably to a certain kind of experience for that sex, more of an affective than a cognitive nature, and that this experience is interwoven with social learning, contributing in a major way to personality development, including self concept, and thus to behavioral differences between the sexes. Freud's explanation, which embodies the whole theory of psychosexual development, was more complex than that stemming from the theory of innate biology or social learning, but it now appears to be in part a reflection of the patterns of thought prevalent in his times. For example, in associating the passive attitude with the receptivity the female displays in the act of conception, he was relating biological function to psychological characteristic. Evidence from cross-cultural studies and later psychoanalytic observations have since challenged and revised many of Freud's early notions while seeming to confirm the existence of traits which are more or less sex-related. Examples are aggressiveness associated with the male or mothering with the female, that appear to be independent of cultural patterns of the societies in which they are found. Recent sex research has also questioned some of Freud's assumptions, but Stoller feels that it has not wholly disproved the fundamental tenets of Freud's theory.[9]

Developmental aspects in childhood

Despite the fact that gender identity is established early in life, developmental experiences are highly influential in communicating the meaning of being male or female to the individual, in determining the eventual content of gender role concepts, in the forming of adult patterns of personal relationships, and in sexual orientation and behavior. It is important to consider developmental processes which are involved in the formation of a self concept, particularly with regard to femininity and masculinity—in other words, how persons come to define *for themselves* what is masculine or feminine in the course of their own development and how this self concept may affect their adult sexual response.

Because children develop in response to a series of human relationships, the concept of self and of ideal self bears the stamp of the history of these relationships. At birth the infant requires a dependable caretaking relationship in order to survive. This first essential relationship profoundly influences the infant's psychological potentials. Its effect on the innate capacities of the developing infant is so profound that it is difficult to separate in any absolute way those aspects of development that are "biological" from those that are "psychological" or environmental in origin. Actually, development is psychobiological, and biology and psychology proceed together. The caretaking person may in fact be the child's biological mother, but this person may also be the father, another relative, a nurse or an older sibling, or several individuals may share the caretaking functions. The word *mother* will here be used for the person who occupies the chief caretaking role for the child. (Although the feminine gender has been used in the discussion that follows, it is understood that the gender of the caretaking person is probably not important in the first months of life.)

Separation — closeness. The mother's conception of herself in relation to her child will influence her behavior with the child and, in consequence, the child's self concept. If the mother unconsciously conceives of her child as merely an extension of herself, the child may perceive himself or herself as only an extension of the mother. If the mother conceives of the child only in terms of the child's demanding capacities, this will influence the child's concept in the direction of dependency; conversely, if the mother encourages the child's participation in self-care, the child will be influenced to value an inner potential for initiative. Simultaneously, the child is learning about the boundaries between himself or herself and the mother.

At first, the child exists in a symbiotic relationship with the mother which is essential for initial survival; the experiencing of *separateness*, however, is necessary for the child's continued development. Self is differentiated gradually from nonself, followed by development of the concept of a separate self which relates to the mother as another, separate person. Ideally, the mother is able to respond to the child's needs for both closeness and distance. Distance provides the opportunity for *manageable experiences of separation* from the mother—for example, the toddler exploring situations away from mother and returning to her from time to time.[10] Such experiences are essential for continued maturation in which capacities for both separateness and closeness are valued and developed.

The child's image of the mother does not correspond exactly in fact to the mother, but is related to the child's perceptual capacities and needs at various stages of development. Children may attribute qualities to the mother in relation to their own needs and may perceive the mother principally in terms of her capacity to diminish or increase their feeling of tension. Thus, when the child is frustrated and overwhelmed by internal feelings and can be immediately reassured and satisfied by the mother's ministrations, the mother may be experienced as being quite powerful. These caretaking functions then may be viewed as if they were the only functions the mother has.

For both boys and girls these early experiences with the mother provide a basis for their attitudes about women in later life. To the extent that *the mother* feels she has value only in terms of her caretaking capacities, this may reinforce the child's early images of the mother in these terms. These feelings may be internalized, may become unconscious, and in adult life may cause the individual to view women exclusively in terms of their capacity to provide gratification and relieve distress; this, in turn, may determine the adult's expectations about what is "reasonable" in a close relationship. Case vignette 3 involving a parent-child relationship is illustrative:

> Mrs. X, in analysis, discussed her difficulty in getting her 6-year-old son to bed. In order for her to feel like a "good mother," it was necessary that her son not be in conflict with her and agree that he also wished to go to bed. Naturally, he did not always feel this way. She would then engage in a long power struggle and debate often ending in an explosive, punitive outburst on her part which settled the matter but left her feeling "bad" and deserving punishment from the child. This would set the stage for the next cycle when she again would redouble her efforts to be a "good mother."
>
> Mrs. X's own mother had difficulty in being direct with her about her own needs when they conflicted with her daughter's. She relived with her own child her own internalization of the mother-child relationship. To part of her, a "good mother" was only a providing mother with no needs of her own. When conflict arose in her relationship with her child she felt either she had become a "bad mother" or else the child was "bad" for wanting something she did not wish to give. She could only set limits for the child in the context of feeling like a "bad mother." Similarly, she could not feel like a "good mother" if she recognized that it was her fatigue which in part determined her child's bedtime.

Body image and self concept. Children's experiences with their own bodies form the basis for the body image, which, in turn, is the initial basis for the child's self concept.[11] The self concept will thus be influenced by whether or not the body is experienced as a source of pleasure, and also by the response of others in the environment to the child's body and biological functions. In illustration, if the child feels that a particular bodily activity is in danger of being taken over by others outside of the self, such an activity may begin to be viewed in terms of a power struggle. In this way, eating can come to be thought of as belonging outside of the self and subject to regulation for the benefit of others, as can urination and defecation. Failure to allow the child to participate in the regulation of appetite, sleep, defecation, or other bodily function may promote a rather one-sided view of interaction around body experiences. If such patterns persist, all personal relationships may reflect a preoccupation with themes of domination, submission and power, which are then seen as the "norm" of human interaction. More mutually regulated interactions with the parents will favor the possibility of more collaborative modes of relationships in later life. Adult sexual relationships, which involve both bodily activity and response to another person, are affected in many individuals by unconscious residues of these early experiences.

Parental values. Children's feelings about their bodies and themselves also reflect the nature of the family structure and the family's values. In some families, only qualities that are endowed with or represent "maleness" are valued. It should not be surprising, then, that a male child in such a family would tend to consider his penis one of the most important parts of his body, and he might also feel that physical strength, courage and the ability to fight (or whatever the family designates as masculine) are all essential qualities. A female child in such a family might feel that the absence of a penis and of qualities of strength and courage represents a grave liability for her in achieving a sense of value as a person (often referred to in the psychoanalytic literature as penis envy).[12] Similarly, a boy might feel threatened by a lack of these traits, imagined or real, or by any signs of "femaleness" in himself. The girl might overvalue any attribute of herself, such as her clitoris or her physical strength, that could represent for her some form of "maleness"; she might also devalue parts of her personality or her body, such as her vagina, which represent "femaleness" to her.

Or if the child perceives the mother as powerfully dominating the father, "femaleness" may be overvalued. A male child in such a family may be fearful of his own maleness and experience his penis or any representation of his father in himself as a liability. A female child who experiences her mother in these terms may internalize her mother's contempt for maleness and depreciate qualities in herself or others which she identifies as being connected with her father. To sum up, although the process of internalization is part of development for everyone, precisely what gets internalized is highly variable and idiosyncratic for particular children even within the same family, depending on the place of each in the particular family constellation and on the child's perception of the parents.[13]

Identification. The development of the self concept is also profoundly influenced by the process of identification. The first identification for both girls and boys is with the mother and this is an important vehicle for learning as well as an essential for psychological growth. In the girl's development, this primary identification with her mother is consonant with a female gender identity. However, as a basis for future heterosexual orientation, she must shift some of her initial attachment from her mother to her father.* For the boy, an attachment to his mother is consistent with his presumed future sexual orientation but not with gender identity, so that

---

* The term *father* is used for simplicity; in the absence of the natural father, the same function may be performed by some other significant male.

he must achieve some distance from his initial identification with his mother, form an attachment to his father, and shift to a principal identification with his father.[14]

The boy's identification with his father is facilitated when the mother values the father and his male qualities. The boy, through his identification with his mother's attitudes, can then value his own masculinity. Similarly the girl is assisted in her attachment to her father by identifying with her mother's interest in him. The emotional availability of the father is important for the boy to assist his identification as a male, and for the girl in her self-definition as a female. Both boys and girls to some extent internalize both parents' views of femininity and masculinity.

Because the child has attachments to both parents and at times wishes to have an exclusive arrangement with one, the child will also feel varying degrees of competition and rivalry with the parent of the same sex (referred to as oedipal feelings). This inevitable rivalry is usually strongest with the parent of the same sex but is not restricted to this parent alone. The resolution of these conflicting feelings is an important determinant of the child's emerging personality and sexual development. The parent of the same sex, however, is not always the principal rival. In some families, it is the mother for the boy or the father for the girl. In other situations, the absence, or the perceived ineffectuality, of the parent of the same sex can lead to a void in the child's experience with competition. Under such circumstances, the child may aggrandize his or her self-worth but, because no actual test of competition ever takes place, may develop a paradoxical sense of special superiority along with a simultaneous conviction of vulnerability.

The child is not only envious of, but is also relieved and supported in growth by, the strength of the parents' attachment to each other. A strong attachment between the parents facilitates the development of extrafamilial attachments to

peers and frees the child's energy for growth as a more autonomous person. The child is relieved to know that, however
much he or she wishes it, there will never actually have to be a
final confrontation with one parent in a life-and-death battle
for the other. To a degree, of course, the boy needs his mother
to respond to his maleness just as the girl needs her father to
respond to her femaleness.[15] This response gives each one the
confidence to attract a sexual partner, later on, among peers.
The absence of such responsiveness on the part of the parent,
or an overexaggerated response, can pose problems for the
child.

Anxieties and conflicts. During the phase of development between the ages of three and five, feelings about the penis and
the qualities it symbolizes may be important to the child.
When these feelings persist into adulthood, problems arise.
Thus, the male may compare himself to a "phallic ideal,"
expecting himself to be Superman defined in terms of the
qualities of an erect penis (hard-driving, "on the make").
Feelings that do not fit this ideal, such as tenderness and
compassion, may be felt as threats, engendering low self-
esteem or a sense of emasculation. Correspondingly, the
female may compare herself with a related ideal which is
oriented toward the absence of phallic qualities (being soft,
yielding, unassertive). This ideal leaves her vulnerable to the
feeling that self-interest, initiative and competence are masculine qualities, which may threaten her sense of femininity to
the extent that she demonstrates them.

At another extreme, the man may have difficulty integrating into his self-image his potential for self-assertion and
strength *because* he associates these qualities internally with
masculinity, which may evoke fears of retaliation (referred to
as castration anxiety). Similarly for the woman, the integration of receptive or tender feelings may also be a problem
when she identifies these qualities as feminine, which she can
also perceive as threatening. In other words, some men and

some women may experience anxiety about both "feminine" and "masculine" qualities in themselves, depending on how these qualities have been defined for them in early life. Case example 4 illustrates difficulties arising from failure to resolve such conflicts:

> Mr. Y, a 32-year-old, very successful and depressed lawyer in analysis, responded to helpful comments from the analyst with self-criticism and feelings of inadequacy. He felt himself inferior in relation to the analyst's insights, and he attributed a power to the analyst which was in part a replica of his feelings about his father, whom he also endowed with an almost magical sense of potency. He measured himself against this ideal, to which he equated the analyst, and felt impotent when he experienced the analyst as more capable than himself.
>
> At the same time, Mr. Y viewed sensitivity and awareness as feminine, belonging to the women in his family. For him, anything other than activity was viewed as feminine, so he felt threatened by his potential for self-awareness. For varying reasons, he felt anxious when he was helped by the analyst in the analysis. It threatened his sense of masculinity to be helped and to be reminded that he was not his omnipotent ideal. He projected onto the analyst both an aspect of himself, which he regarded as feminine, and at the same time his super masculine ideal. The analysis enabled him to develop a different ideal for himself which could encompass and also value qualities of sensitivity and self-awareness that might conventionally be interpreted as feminine, as well as activity and mastery.

A further contribution to the sense of one's self as an adult, particularly as a sexual person, is made by the child's perception of the parents' relationship with each other, interpreting from this perception what it is to be a wife or a husband. Even children who consciously reject their parents as models are nevertheless influenced by exposure to them, for the experience is internalized unconsciously. This contributes to the child's ideal self concept—that is, the sense of how one *ought* or *ought not* to be as a spouse.[16] Parental interaction will reveal some of the parents' own internalizations of maleness and femaleness, and through repeated observations the child will surmise something about the essence of the parental relationship, including some notions about the parents' sexual life, whether actually witnessed or not. Such fantasies may represent in succinct short-hand form the child's image of the intimate parental relationship which may be represented in a variety of ways—as intrusive, aggressive, cooperative, assaultive, tender, or whatever, depending on the particular relationship between the parents and how it is experienced by the child. Often such childhood imagery is lived out in intimate relationships and sexual experiences in later life, as case vignette 5 illustrates:

> Mrs. Z, a young woman who consciously sought a more gratifying and egalitarian sexual partnership, nonetheless reported in her treatment that she "collaborated" in assaultive rape-like sexual attacks by her husband. Her childhood was filled with accounts by her mother of her father's brutishness and she identified with her mother's view of her father. She conceived of her parents' sexual experiences as ones in which her father intrusively and brutally attacked her mother.
>
> Without being aware of it, Mrs. Z was reliving this conception of her parents' relationship in her marriage and unwittingly encouraging her husband to act out this imagery with her although it conflicted with her consciously held concepts of what she wanted.

The child is also subject to influences outside the home, and of course internalizes concepts from the culture, not only about how to be a person, but also about gender role. In children's experience with others outside the home, they may become aware of different models for being a person and also different definitions of masculinity and femininity. These models influence the child's ideal self concept, which in turn will affect the child's self-esteem. Children measure themselves against idealized representations of masculinity or femininity and experience a gain or loss of self-esteem insofar as these ideals are or are not reached.

Developmental aspects in adolescence

With the onset of puberty, the changes associated with the development of secondary sexual characteristics take place and must be integrated with all the internalized residues from preceding developmental phases, that is, with the conscious and unconscious prior evolution of self concept, sexuality, and impressions about gender role. Thus, for some children the emergence of bodily changes representing further self-definition as a sexual person may evoke considerable anxiety, while for others such changes may be welcome and non-threatening. The onset of menstruation in girls and the development of the capacity for ejaculation in boys are not only physiological changes—they also have psychological correlates—and the meaning assigned to each will be influenced by the individual's previous self concept. A girl who has internalized a depreciated view of women or of herself may regard menstruation as the expression of her "badness," and her menstrual fluid as visible evidence of "bad stuff" in her. In contrast, a girl with a more favorable view of women may view menstruation as a step toward the status of a grown woman and so respond positively. Bodily configurations such as size of breasts or penis, shape of hips, amount of fat, and so on assume importance in relation to the symbolic meaning which the adolescent assigns to these body parts. Issues of self-worth tend to be linked to these bodily changes, the impact of which will vary, depending on the adolescent's ideal.

In adolescence, the principal task of development centers on efforts to consolidate a mature sense of personal identity, and considerable experimenting with a variety of consciously chosen self concepts may precede such consolidation. These efforts may conflict with unconscious residues from childhood. Old concepts of selfhood and identity are not and cannot be discarded simply by choosing a new way of defining oneself. The outcome of these identity struggles during adolescence does not always conform to some cultural ideal. Rather, as in every phase of development, adolescents attempt to find some way of integrating different aspects of themselves with alternative models perceived in the environment. In each phase of development certain critical conflicts arise, the outcome of which will affect the next developmental phase, and in every subsequent phase there is some overlap and reworking of what has gone before. Change itself may provoke anxiety, but many psychiatrists believe that some conflict and disturbance are part of the norm of healthy development and actually lead to further growth.

In summary, the internalized and ideal self concepts exert an important influence on the organization of behavior in the developing individual. The vitally important feeling of self-worth is dependent on the extent to which one's self concept approximates the ideal self. Each stage of development, beginning in infancy and continuing throughout the life cycle, makes important contributions to the formation of the self-image. Development of the concept of male and female gender roles is often seen as consisting of opposing traits, and a definition of one implies a definition of the other. Often these traits are related to sexual behavior.

Sexual orientation, behavior, and gender role

Because the one unequivocal event involving anatomical and physiological difference between a male and a female is the sexual act of reproduction, sexual behavior in its various aspects has at times been used to define the quintessential characteristics of maleness and femaleness. Qualities necessary to perform the sexual act, such as the male's penetration and thrust or the female's receptiveness, have been generalized and applied to all sorts of situations to define masculine or feminine behavior. Thus, the individual's sexual response and orientation have been viewed as closely related to concepts of masculinity and femininity. Recent research, however, has challenged the normative premise of such a definition and has prompted questions about stereotypes of masculinity and femininity in sexual as well as nonsexual matters. However, because it is difficult for most individuals to separate issues of gender role from feelings about sexual response, such considerations remain psychologically important.

As already noted, recent studies of animal development have stressed the effect of early biological and social conditions on adult sexual response. Because of methodological problems, sexual behavior in human beings, however, is probably the most difficult aspect of male and female behavior to document. Restrictions on experiments involving human subjects limit some sources of data. Case histories and subjective impressions or recollections, which are prominent sources of data, are open to the usual criticisms regarding their reliability and representative character. The extensive experimental work of recent years has added vast and rich material, but questions still arise owing to the artificiality of laboratory conditions and the nature of the sampling (which is largely dependent on volunteer subjects).

Traits, both specific and general, which traditionally have been ascribed to gender have been compared for females and males and statistical differences found. These include differences in aggressivity, in interests (inner space vs outer space), in physical durability, special aptitudes (intuitive vs analytical), concern with predictability of the environment (preservers vs experimenters), sensory perception, and rate of maturation both mental and physical. It has not been made clear, however, whether the differences found are rooted in biology or social conditioning. Kinsey added an observation that males appear to have a greater capacity to be conditioned by sexual experience and to establish associative links between sexual and nonsexual substitutive stimuli.[17] Through the work of Masters and Johnson, the last decade has been characterized by an enormous concentration of attention on the orgasm.[18] One of the important possibilities they inferred was that females, in contrast to males, may be naturally multiorgasmic. Overall, however, these investigators have emphasized the remarkable physiological *similarities* between male and female sexual response.

During intrauterine life the genital anlage in female and male embryos gradually evolves into ovary and testes, clitoris and penis. It does not seem unlikely to assume that the experience of a visible, palpable organ for the boy must differ from that of the girl, who discovers her own genitals more gradually by sensation and exploration. These anatomical differences represent the most highly specific biological distinctions between the sexes until puberty, when patterns of sexual hormone production begin to vary. These patterns are felt to be related to sexual responsiveness as well as to secondary sex characteristics. The specified effects of the individual hormones are complex, but the pattern of hormonal activity may exert differential pressures on the behavior of boys and girls as well as affecting their physical development.

Another important differentiating biological factor is the male accumulation of seminal fluid, which will be discharged periodically through active efforts of the male by masturbation, intercourse or other outlet or, in the absence of action, by spontaneous nocturnal emission. Secretions are a product of female sexual arousal but constitute a phenomenon very dif-

ferent from seminal fluid. The mechanism of sexual desire is
poorly understood,[19] but motivation for orgasm may be more
of a physiological mandate for males early in adolescence
(males are observed to engage in masturbation more frequently) and may continue more or less as a steady state, while
for females it may more often depend on learned
experience—although it is also possible that underlying
biological need has been inhibited in the female by developmental influences and simply needs to be released. One finding used to reinforce this possibility is that males reach a peak
of orgasmic activity about a decade earlier than females.
There is presently, however, no method of determining
whether this difference is due to biological or social factors.

One might speculate that, if the difference is primarily a
matter of social conditioning, current changes in attitudes
toward sexuality may lead to a shift in these findings, but it is
too soon to have amassed sufficient indicative empirical data.
On the other hand, if the difference is essentially biological,
this would tend to confirm the role of pursuer, aggressor and
initiator as in fact related to being male. Physiologists and
biochemists may well be able to add significantly to this sketch
of obvious biological differences between the sexes, and indeed their findings may some day provide the essential data
required for a better understanding of sexuality and its place
in the context of personality development. Let us meanwhile
turn briefly to a few of the many beliefs about female
sexuality.

The beliefs about female sexuality are simply accepted
generalizations based on some evidence and some theory.
One important belief is that there is a gestalt of feminine
qualities having to do with a tendency to look inward. Erikson
postulated the concept of "inner space" based on the role of
the woman in the period of gestation during which a child
grows inside her.[20] Another belief is that in regard to sexual
activity the woman takes a greater interest in a full relation-

ship with another person than in the specific act of intercourse. By implication, sexual expression is thought to be
more dependent in females than in males on an experience of
love or a romantic illusion about love. Related to this is the
seeming diffusion of sexual feelings in the female to the
totality of the sexual experience and to her total body as
contrasted with the male's apparently greater tendency to
focus on genital sensations and orgasm. The pervasiveness of
sexual feelings in the female is associated variously—with the
spread of erotic sensations from the genital region to the
whole body, with the special aspects of self-love, and with the
opportunity for the girl to preserve unconscious representations of the body-caretaking mother. These feelings contrast
with those of the boy, who must establish distance from such
maternal internalizations in order to achieve a separate masculine identity. If these feelings really are gender-related,
they clearly would influence the emotional attitudes that men
and women bring not only to the sexual act, but to the
relationship.

Another set of "female" traits is deduced from various
stages in the process of reproduction, that is, the configura-
tion of the sexual act, the fact of conception, the process of
gestation, and breast-feeding of the infant. Thus *for the female,*
from the sexual act are deduced the qualities of being accepting, receptive and perhaps submissive; from conception, in-
corporativeness; from gestation, nurturance; and from
breast-feeding, nurturance, closeness and giving. *For the male,*
from the sexual act are deduced activity, pursuit, aggressiveness, conquest, directness, and thrust; and from the remaining stages, the ability to protect and provide for a mate (a
female) and children.

From the same general source but more abstractly derived,
a characteristic frequently attributed to the female is a greater devotion to the principles and practice of monogamy and
fidelity. While this quality may be more a wish than an actual-

ity, it has been assumed by many that the woman, because of her role responsibilities as mother and nurturer of the helpless infant, tends to be the guardian of the family unit and the arbiter of morality. For her to ignore these responsibilities is to risk disruption of the family. This view may in part be deduced from observations on primates, among whom the mother clearly assumes these roles. Again, these concepts are frequently employed to determine the "appropriate" or "natural" role of women.

Historically in American society, adulterous behavior has been condemned more sharply in the woman than in the man; similarly, desertion or neglect of the family has been regarded as more offensive in the female than in the male. This probably relates to the view of the mother as nurturer and perhaps also to the property concept in marriage. Recently the opinion has been expressed that the standard of fidelity in women was devised by men to constrain women and preserve male dominance while permitting men to enjoy their own infidelities if they were so inclined. On the other hand, until the development of reliable methods of contraception it was the woman who incurred the potentially serious consequences of pregnancy if she engaged in sexual intercourse outside of marriage. In the last few years, attitudes have emerged which reflect the growing disenchantment with the double standard. Ironically, our society, while conventionally intolerant of infidelity, promotes and propagandizes its forerunners: flirtation, body exposure, alcohol, and other devices to decrease sexual inhibition. The female body and the female mystique are emphasized for the explicit purpose of whetting the male sexual appetite, and the very concept of seductiveness is usually associated with woman. The man is portrayed as eternally eager to engage in the sex act, and his alleged proclivity is symbolized by animal synonyms (stud, wolf, stag). There is more than a little evidence to suggest that such beliefs are assimilated by men and women in the process of growing up and that their behavior is often affected by their attempts to live up to an assumed gender ideal.

Sexual behavior, then, is not a clear-cut phenomenon. It is a mix of physiology and anatomy, of emotions, attitudes and expectations of one individual reacting with a similar mix in another individual. This interaction will be modified by various pressures from the broader surrounding milieu, itself influenced by precedent from the past, change in the present, and interest in the future. At best, all these elements blend into an experience that is satisfying, without being harmful, to men and women singly or as a group. The tide of opinion seems to be in the direction of greater permissiveness toward sexual expression, at least in the middle and upper middle-class levels of our society.

Female sexual response and behavior are becoming better understood and are probably on the whole less different from male sexual response and behavior than had been thought. Certainly there are differences, but those within each gender group appear far more significant than those between the sexes. Among women, affects, behaviors and goals differ enormously and overlap those within the wide spectrum considered characteristic for men. It is important to keep this in mind, for it cannot be overstressed that there is a wide range of affects, behavior and goals in both sexes, which makes rigid definitions inappropriate and restrictive. Yet, as already noted, women—and men—are frequently encumbered in a particular action or feeling by the fact that it does not meet some prevailing criterion of acceptability for their sex.

Whether the concepts, masculinity and femininity, are of any practical use is questionable, but a study of human societies supports the view that these concepts are universal. Therefore, the important question is, what consequences flow from these concepts as they exist in our society?

One potential outcome of sexual behavior that is unique to women is pregnancy and childbirth. For this reason maternity is frequently seen as quintessential to womanliness and by inference to a sense of fulfillment "as a woman." This creates a most complicated, controversial and as yet unsettled issue. It has yet to be determined whether the experiences that make for fulfillment for the majority of women are related to biological capacity, specifically the ability to produce a child. There are two general views about this issue: The first is that the capacity to bear a child is so central to a woman's being that her physiological potential is felt as a psychological drive. Admittedly, some women do not want to have children, but such women are considered to be "unusual" and although individuals among their number may achieve personal fulfillment, there is always the implication that it was achieved in adaptation to potentially neurotic tendencies. The second view is that a woman's fulfillment should be achieved "as a person," which bypasses any suggestion that factors central to this fulfillment are necessarily based on her anatomy. Obviously, the two views are not an either-or proposition, but at times they are so stated. Somewhere between them lies the inescapable fact that the physiological capacity to have children, whether or not felt as a psychological drive, is something every woman must come to terms with—as a risk, a choice, or a fulfillment.

Inevitably this controversy becomes embroiled in a teleological concern. Adherents of the first view point out that, if the view of woman's fulfillment "as a person" really gained sway and no woman chose to bear children, the species would become extinct and there would be no more women to be fulfilled. Proponents of the second view reply that, while this argument is logical, it is highly unlikely that all women will choose not to bear children and therefore equally unlikely that the species will die out in consequence. Because it is only recently that, given the presumption of a certain amount of sexual activity, women really had the ability to prevent conception, the problem is a new one. Presumably such discussions concern matters of individual psychology and should not be influenced by matters of social policy; however, with the realization of the consequences of overpopulation and the emergence of the ZPG (Zero Population Growth) movement, there seems to have been a shift in the attitude that maternity is a necessary condition for female fulfillment. Thus there exists a suspicion that some of the views about the woman's "innate" desire to have children are unconscious feelings and currently illogical attitudes about propagating the race. Should this suspicion be confirmed, it will be necessary to review many of the tenets of female psychology. At this juncture, it is still an open question.

REFERENCES

1. WEBSTER'S THIRD NEW INTERNATIONAL DICTIONARY, unabridged (Springfield, Mass.: G. & C. Merriam, 1966).
2. John Money. "Hermaphroditism," in THE ENCYCLOPEDIA OF SEXUAL BEHAVIOR, Albert Ellis & Albert Abarbanel, Eds. (New York: Hawthorn Books, 1961) Vol 1, pp 472-484.
3. Webster, op. cit.
4. John Money & Anke A. Ehrhardt. MAN & WOMAN, BOY & GIRL (Baltimore: The Johns Hopkins University Press, 1972).
5. Margaret Mead. SEX AND TEMPERAMENT IN THREE PRIMITIVE SOCIETIES (New York: William Morrow, 1935).
6. Warren J. Gadpaille. Research into the Physiology of Maleness and Femaleness, Archives of General Psychiatry 26 (1972): 193-206.
7. Ibid.
8. Leonore Tiefer. Commentary on "Innate Masculine-Feminine Differences," Medical Aspects of Human Sexuality 7 (1973): 156-157.
9. Robert J. Stoller. Overview: The Impact of New Advances in Sex Research on Psychoanalytic Theory, American Journal of Psychiatry 130 (1973): 241-251.
10. Margaret S. Mahler & Manuel Furer. Certain Aspects of the Separation-Individuation Phase, Psychoanalytic Quarterly 32:(1963): 1-14.
11. Willie Hoffer. Development of the Body Ego, Psychoanalytic Study of the Child 5 (1950): 18-23.

12. W. G. Joffe. A Critical Review of the Status of the Envy Concept, *International Journal of Psychoanalysis* 50 (1969): 533-545.
13. Roy Schafer. ASPECTS OF INTERNALIZATION (New York: International Universities Press, 1968).
14. Ralph R. Greenson. Dis-identifying from Mother: Its Special Importance for the Boy, *International Journal of Psychoanalysis* 49 (1968): 370-374.
15. M. Leonard. Fathers and Daughters, *International Journal of Psychoanalysis* 47 (1966): 325-334.
16. Joseph Sandler, Alex Holder & Dale Meers. The Ego Ideal and the Ideal Self, *Psychoanalytic Study of the Child* 18 (1963): 139-159.
17. Alfred C. Kinsey, Wardell B. Pomeroy, Clyde E. Martin & Paul H. Gebhard. SEXUAL BEHAVIOR IN THE HUMAN MALE (Philadelphia: Saunders, 1948).
18. William H. Masters & Virginia E. Johnson. HUMAN SEXUAL RESPONSE (Boston: Little, Brown, 1966).
19. Lester A. Kirkendall. "Sex Drive," in THE ENCYCLOPEDIA OF SEXUAL BEHAVIOR Albert Ellis & Albert Abarbanel, Eds. (New York: Hawthorn Books, 1961) Vol 2, pp 939-948.
20. Erik H. Erikson. "Inner and Outer Space: Reflections on Womanhood," in THE WOMAN IN AMERICA (Boston: Beacon Press, 1967) pp 1-26.

5

COLLEGE AND AFTER

In late adolescence or early adulthood, roughly the college period, one of the most important and perhaps difficult tasks of the growing individual is the simultaneous development of autonomy and a satisfactory sexual orientation. Becoming an independent, self-governing individual and at the same time establishing one's ability to relate to another person sexually is a major task requiring resources uncompromised by disabling conflicts. Issues of dependence and independence are involved which are often difficult to integrate satisfactorily. Most young people go through a process of emancipation from their parental family on the one hand, while on the other they experiment with a variety of emotional and/or sexual relationships. The primary purpose of college is academic, but it is generally recognized that college also provides the setting for important advances in personality development.[1] For most college men and women, this means establishing some reasonably settled view of oneself as an individual and some capacity for intimacy.

Development of gender role

Except for a few colleges, at which education of "the total person" is an active goal, most colleges do not offer their students much that directly contributes to the development of gender role. To the extent that the college indirectly provides some structure which can be utilized in the development of identity, those traits traditionally associated with maleness appear to be those most likely to be effectively encouraged.

For example, the pursuit of a career with single-minded determination in a highly competitive atmosphere where most of the teaching is done by a male faculty is more compatible to students with conventionally masculine than feminine characteristics. To compete successfully in such a milieu, the woman often must be aggressive and must actively combat bias on the part of male teachers—a bias sometimes expressed by covert or overt refusal to take the woman student seriously.

At the same time, the male student has usually been given the opportunity and sanction for direct sexual experience which would favor the integration of his sexual orientation, whereas the woman has not been given like opportunity, at least in times past. Thus it is the man who has more opportunities during his four years in college to undergo experiences which assist both his autonomous development and the establishment of his sexual orientation. Although he may as a result show evidence of great turmoil during his college years, he is the more likely upon graduation to have consolidated and synthesized his personality to a considerable extent.

The woman student experiences college differently. Although she may engage in sexual experimentation, the psychological development required for her reproductive role (pregnancy, childbearing and early childrearing) is usually not confronted in a preparatory or anticipatory way, either directly or indirectly, and frequently not even intellectually to any significant degree. The college environment is actually antipathetic to such development because if the woman is a serious student she will usually not have the time or the opportunity. Career development, multiplicity of job choices, and varying options in life style may be important for her autonomous development, but they will not favor resolution of conscious or unconscious conflicts about her sexual and reproductive role. In fact, the pressure for outstanding intellectual performance may serve as a defense against undertaking the arduous task of developing a capacity for sexual intimacy. This is not to suggest that wholehearted involvement in intellectual activities is neurotic or precludes development in the sexual sphere, but it should be recognized that pursuit of a career can offer an escape from sexual anxiety and conflicts.

Conversely, undue reliance on sexual activity as a form of gratification can interfere with the development of other capacities that may be needed later in life. The extremes of such one-sided development are caricatured in the brilliant, competent and successful woman essentially sealed off from her instinctual life, who is emotionally cold and often angry with men, representing one extreme; and the attractive, popular, seductive girl seemingly shallow, dependent and "dumb," who is related to by men solely as a sex object, at the opposite extreme.

Case vignette 6 is an example from the psychoanalysis of a woman who entered therapy in her late thirties.

> Mrs. A sought help because of severe phobias which restricted her movement away from home and precluded her professional travel. Issues were raised in the analysis of Mrs. A that traced some of her difficulties to a failure to resolve problems of autonomy and gender role. She was a capable student, elected to Phi Beta Kappa when she graduated from college. When she showed her father her Phi Beta Kappa Key he said, "With that and 10 cents you can get a ride on the subway." This incident was characteristic of many experiences in which she felt her father demeaned her intellectual achievements. For Mrs. A, the "mind" was a masculine prerogative, particularly skills relating to mathematics or mechanical things. On the other hand, historical or more abstract pursuits, which she herself viewed as ineffectual, were permissively feminine, and she had taken a Ph.D. degree in such a field.
>
> In her analysis, Mrs. A appreciated more fully that her father was threatened by her intellectual capacities, and she

behaved as if her vitality belonged to a male part of herself. She felt that she would be unfeminine or potentially castrating to men if she were openly to show her intellectual potential. She had been able to work only at scholarly tasks which she regarded as highly obscure or "dead." She was restricted in applying her competence to more active or action-oriented fields. In addition, her mother had overestimated her capabilities and she felt that she was expected to perform in order to make up for her mother's emptiness, to supply the mother with her missing male part which at the same time threatened her father.

This struggle was being waged internally and was one source of Mrs. A's marked inhibitions and phobias. She had great difficulty asking her husband directly to accommodate her own career when it might inconvenience him. Internally, she also experienced herself as "bad" when she acted outside of her internalized model for femininity in which there was no channel for developing an autonomous self.

In their college years most students will experience relationships of an emotional nature with some degree of attachment to another individual. Sexual experimentation is likely to occur and may or may not involve intercourse. For some, the experience will be fleeting—a single date or a series of brief encounters; for others, the relationship may be serious and may last for an indefinite period. Attachments may be of a homosexual or heterosexual nature. Most individuals will opt for a heterosexual orientation, but for some a homosexual orientation may represent the orientation of choice.* In either case the opportunity exists to learn how one's self concept, gender identity, and sexual responsiveness work in actual practice. In arriving at an adult sexual orientation,

* In the ensuing discussion we have primarily focused on heterosexual relationships because, besides being statistically most likely, they inevitably highlight issues relating to gender differences.

patterns of sexual relationships, both heterosexual and homosexual, may become exceedingly complex and will inevitably be affected by earlier developmental events, identifications and conflicts. It is not uncommon to find a person repeating experiences directly connected with unconscious images of masculinity and femininity formed during earlier periods of development long forgotten, while the conscious effort is to impose new self-definitions. Thus, persons who reject the nuclear family in favor of communal living may nevertheless replicate in this new life style patterns of behavior resembling those of their own early parental models that they have tried so hard to replace.

There are many life styles which reflect different concepts of masculinity and femininity. Certain of these life styles will be more adaptive for some persons than for others. This will depend on how well any particular pattern, whether or not a socially conventional one, represents the best possible resolution of the diverse and sometimes conflicting interests of the individual. From a psychoanalytic viewpoint, a style is adaptive to the extent that the behavior elected takes into account the internal as well as the external realities of the person. *Adaptive* does not mean simply conforming to a social norm or even necessarily behaving "logically," although these may be among the adaptive requirements of a particular life style. Adaptation might involve a capacity to change the environment or to search out a new and more favorable environment. No single life style can be presumed *a priori* to be "healthier" or "more adaptive" for all persons. What is adaptive may not only differ from one person to another, but may also change for any given person as development proceeds throughout the life cycle. Case vignette 7 illustrates some of these points:

> Jane was a senior student working toward completion of her honors thesis. She had a strong interest in math and physical science and generally did well. She had been supported by her professors and her thesis adviser in this work,

although she had had a number of near-arguments with her
adviser in which she felt he was not taking her seriously
enough, and had not given her sufficient credit for her
independence of thought. Jane was concerned that as a
woman she was not expected to make use of her math and
physics skills in the future. It was very important to her to
"amount to something" and to attain prominence in her
field, yet she was very sensitive to any implications that
might challenge her "femininity."

Jane's boyfriend was also a science student, in graduate
school. Recently they had talked of getting married. She felt
in considerable conflict—felt that she might be unfair to him
if they did get married, despite her strong conviction that a
two-career family was possible. Actually he was very supportive of her working after marriage, as several women in his
family had professional careers.

Jane came for counseling help after she blew up when a
professor questioned her on a point of data. She felt she had
overreacted, and that her sensitivity threatened the possibility of obtaining a fellowship. She described the ways in
which "the system" worked to the disadvantage of women
students, the overt and covert discrimination. She also recognized how quick she was to feel threatened or attacked,
and her great sensitivity to depreciation and slights. The
psychiatrist asked her whether she might not share the
ambivalence toward achievement she so readily saw in
others.

Jane was an attractive, lively girl. She had always been the
good student in her family, the youngest of 4 children. Her
mother, a middle-class housewife, had played down Jane's
intellectual achievements although proud of her good rec-
ord at school. She used to tell Jane not to be a "bookworm,"
not to read so much—the boys wouldn't like it. Jane's father
was an unsuccessful but intelligent businessman. For years
he was submerged in work. When he was home or at family
gatherings, he would speak mostly to other men, including
Jane's boyfriend. Her mother deferred to her father, insist-
ing that she couldn't follow the abstract conversations, and
retreated to the kitchen. Jane vowed she would not be like

her mother. She would succeed beyond her father's attainments. She worried that marriage might be a trap, but at the same time felt genuinely drawn to her boyfriend.

After several counseling interviews, Jane saw the degree to which she herself had internalized her family attitude that intellectual achievement would be aggressive, improper and unfeminine. She herself had doubts about her competence. However, her awareness of the intensity of her self-doubt made her less vulnerable to implied criticism from others. A fellow student commented that she seemed less abrasive and provocative of late.

Getting to know the family of a woman professor helped Jane envision the possibility of a kind of marriage different from that of her parents. When she went to visit her family for a holiday, she felt acutely conscious of her mother's sense of entrapment. But this led her to feel some sympathy for her mother and less of the alienation she had felt before. The deeper sources of her self-doubt were not explored, but were acknowledged. Nevertheless, she functioned more comfortably and completed her work.

Each individual must integrate the experience gained from emotional relationships with others into the process of establishing himself or herself as an autonomous person, and these two processes are by no means unrelated. It is not uncommon for the woman (or man) to transfer dependent feelings directly from parents to partner, which often places strains on the relationship that it cannot endure. For this or for other reasons, relationships may develop rapidly and end just as rapidly. Sometimes the relationship may be opportunistic or convenient and fade when circumstances change. Through experience, however, each individual learns something about his or her emotional and sexual response which can make succeeding relationships more satisfactory. For some individuals, of course, unconscious factors will determine the outcome, and these factors are not likely to be neutralized simply by successive experiences.

Although, in the past, relationships between young adults were usually developed through a series of courting rituals such as dates and dances, and exposure to one another prior to engagement was rather artificial, today it is not unusual for a couple to decide to live together for a time without any permanent commitment. In some ways this is a preview of marriage which as such may give the couple the chance to test out their reactions to each other in a very intense way. Presumably such a relationship is most likely to be successful where both partners have been able before that time to achieve a certain autonomy, a capacity for intimacy, and a satisfactory sexual response. If not, this new arrangement may represent a continuation of an effort to remain dependent, with the lover substituted for the parents.

Career and marriage

Not unnaturally, as a male-female relationship develops, the issue of permanence may arise. Traditionally for many, the end of college has been a logical time to consider marriage.* Formerly most women felt themselves faced with a choice between a serious career commitment involving professional or graduate school and a marriage involving full-time motherhood at least for some years. Those few women who chose to combine marriage with a career had to struggle with difficult decisions during the years when many of their friends were having babies. They faced the dilemma whether to work discontinuously, interrupting their work for a few years to have children, or to continue work during this period, and make do with various complicated arrangements for household help and child care.

---

* It is recognized that nowadays a permanent relationship does not necessarily imply marriage. The term *marriage* is used here because many of its implications are so clear-cut. But much of the discussion that follows would apply equally to a non-legalized relationship that the partners considered permanent.

Until recently the combination of career involving continuous work *and* marriage has been the unusual choice for women. But the need to choose between one or the other of these life patterns seems unfortunate. It tends to polarize the marital sphere into the home for women and the outside world for men. It is based on the assumption that there is no way of integrating the pleasures and responsibilities of bringing up children with serious career involvement. For the past few years more students have been electing a relatively uninterrupted working pattern while attempting to work out some pattern of marital living that will make this possible.

The issue of marriage must be dealt with because marriage is still the most accepted choice for most women. Although there is currently some evidence of a trend toward remaining single, the overwhelming majority of women today are married or would like to be. Marriage provides companionship, which is important to most people; it provides a stable environment for raising children, which most women want to have; and it meets the needs of women for protection and security. It also meets the needs of men for companionship and domestic support. Despite the literary convention that men are reluctant bridegrooms, the man in many instances presses the woman to enter marriage. Most college women contemplating the future, however, want both marriage and career. The oft-cited lack of models for women considering a career is in part due to the fact that many career women of the last generation did not marry, and college women tend to dismiss them as models on this account (although there may be some change currently). The assumption underlying their attitude is that either the older woman was unable to achieve marriage, in which case the student doesn't want to identify with her; or, if single by choice, she has excluded a family, which the student is not usually willing to do, at least not at the outset.

Although a stable and fulfilling marriage with mutuality of

relationships has many adaptive functions, particularly in relation to the children, the role of mother-housewife also may
serve defensive purposes. In the process of being a "feminine"
woman and a "good" mother, a woman may effectively isolate
herself from the competitive world, an isolation which may be
encouraged by underlying fears, for example, anxiety about
competing. It may not be necessary or desirable to face such
fears head on yet her choice can be seen to have been influenced by unconscious as well as conscious factors. This may
not become a problem until later in life when her children are
grown and the homemaker role may become less adaptive. At
that time her anxieties may make it difficult to select another
life style even in the face of conscious desire to make a change.

Competitive rivalry with siblings, a parent or other family
member provides the earliest basis for feelings which are later
revived and reinforced by a variety of social situations. In
some degree such feelings are universal but are expressed in
very different ways by different individuals. The girl who has
handled her competitive feelings with her brother by submissiveness, or who has repressed her feelings of rivalry with her
mother in the process of resolving her oedipal feelings may
develop strong inhibitions about expressing aggression later
in her life. She may feel disturbed when confronted with a
type of work which demands personal competition from her,
as Matina Horner has noted.[2] Horner shows in studies done at
Harvard and Michigan that women fear success. Although
later studies have questioned some of her results,[3] fear of
success seems to be a factor in a rather complex reaction.[4,5] A
similar study of men by Lois Hoffman revealed that men also
have anxieties but of a quite different nature.[6] In contrast to
most men, college women associate academic success with
negative consequences. Men may have to cope with similar
anxieties about competition and the expression of aggression,
but they are supported in such behavior by the social values
which make the aggressive, competitive man the ideal. A

woman who chooses the socially acceptable role of full-time wife and mother may be removing herself in this way from confrontation with unresolved conflicts. She has, as well, found an acceptable context in which she can maintain a certain degree of dependency, and dependency may be important to her psychological balance.

Similarly, there are both positive and defensive aspects to choosing a career. A career provides possibilities for the development of intellectual, social and other skills, but it may not be motivated solely by a desire for fulfillment and the development of one's potential. Defensive needs may also be served, for a career permits a woman to avoid the areas of traditional femininity, which may be fraught with conflict arising from her previous life experiences. She may be apprehensive about her sexual functioning and about her capacity to "be a woman," which she visualizes as the ability to bear and raise children and to avoid the mistakes she may feel her own mother has made. This is not to say that the motivation for either choice is "neurotic" but rather that choice is rarely a simple matter—and it is determined by many factors, some adaptive and some defensive.

In any relationship between people, each person's needs are important. For men as well as women, a socially acceptable life pattern may serve defensive purposes. Rigidly held "masculinity" may be a defense against unconscious passive and dependent feelings which would be very threatening if they reached consciousness. A hard-driving businessman who is admired and considered a model of success may also be using his activity to defend against feelings of passivity. In a marriage offering the partners a kind of complementarity from the start, any later change in one partner may create real problems if it disrupts patterns of successful gratification for the other. Thus, if the wife has initially chosen the housewife role and later decides to pursue a career, the marital readjustment may involve far more than simply securing supervi-

sion for the children or a housekeeper to prepare supper.
Case vignette 8 illustrates how the husband may be involved:

> Charles and Dorothy came from relatively wealthy upper
> middle-class families. They were married shortly after
> graduation from college. Charles went to work for a bank at
> a good salary. Dorothy had not followed any career direc-
> tion very seriously in college and was content to establish
> their home and devote herself to volunteer activities of the
> Junior League. Their relationship was a good one. They
> enjoyed several sports together and had a pleasant circle of
> friends. They assumed they would have a child right away
> but Dorothy did not conceive immediately. After the first
> year, she found herself rather restless and not really satis-
> fied by her volunteer activities. Rather unexpectedly she
> was offered a full-time job as an administrative assistant at a
> social agency where she had volunteered and somewhat on
> impulse she accepted it.
>
> At first Charles had no objections and seemed pleased at
> the prospect of increased family income. Gradually, how-
> ever, tensions began to develop in the marriage marked by a
> series of rather heated arguments. Sometimes these spats
> seemed to be about minor matters of housekeeping, such as
> the beds not being made or supper not being ready, and
> sometimes about financial matters, such as the need for a
> new refrigerator, which Dorothy wanted and Charles felt
> was unnecessary. When Dorothy replaced the old one, using
> her own earnings, a really serious fight was precipitated
> which left Charles quite depressed.
>
> Discussion of their tensions with a marriage counselor
> revealed that Charles had a rather rigid concept of marital
> roles. When his role as the provider was threatened by
> Dorothy's earnings and subsequent greater independence,
> his feelings of masculinity were undermined and he found
> himself involuntarily taking positions that were essentially
> irrational. Concomitantly, he found himself inexplicably
> depressed and angry when Dorothy's role as housekeeper,
> cook and sympathetic listener (essentially his mother's role),

which fulfilled his unconscious dependency needs, was altered. The original marital relationship had been a highly
satisfactory one for Charles. When Dorothy changed her
role, he found it difficult to adapt to the new conditions.

Changes in a marital relationship as time passes are almost
inevitable, but some are more difficult to adapt to than others.
Those that modify fundamental patterns of gratifications are
more likely to cause strain.

Pregnancy and the first child

Many factors enter into the ability to adapt to marriage. These
are inevitably complicated further when a child is added. But
once some adaptation to marriage has been made, the next
major change usually involves the decision to have a child. As
long as there are no children, a young couple can function
with relatively loose definition of their roles as husband and
wife. Even when both are students or both work, it is not
particularly difficult to function in a parallel way, to share
household chores, and to enjoy similar goals of personal fulfillment or work commitment.

In this period of marriage there are no necessary contradictions between how the partners work out their life patterns
and conventional expectations. The first pregnancy and the
birth of the first child bring to the marriage an unavoidable
change. The traditional American expectation has been that
the woman will stay at home and care for the child while the
man works to provide financial support. If the tradition is
followed, it represents for the woman a sharper change from
previous marital patterns than for the man. But when the
woman wants to continue to work outside the home, this
represents a break with conventional expectations, which in
itself may create problems.

The experience of pregnancy is one of potential upheaval
as well as gratification for a woman. The first pregnancy

marks a change for her from her role as daughter to that of mother. Her relationship with her own mother is revived —sometimes with a conscious longing for her mother, sometimes with conflicts which make it difficult for her to see herself as a mother. The pregnancy affects her self-image and stirs up problems about her femininity which perhaps have temporarily receded during the previous equilibrium. The responsibility of care for another human being brings a new seriousness to choices about how to live. Once a baby is on its way, there is no turning back from this responsibility. How it will be handled will depend on the future parents, but a couple can no longer make choices about life style as casually or abstractly as before. Old identifications with parental life style are revived and may precipitate conflict with theoretical ideas about how to live that the couple had held unchallenged up to that time. Thus unconscious factors may crucially influence conscious choice. The impact may be more abrupt and far-reaching for the wife, but the husband too may find that his expectations have shifted. Contradictions may arise between his conscious intention of creating a kind of family relationship different from the one he knew and echoes of internalized parental expectations that are unconsciously influencing him to repeat earlier family patterns. Case example 9 illustrates such an unanticipated development:

> During John's early years his father had been almost totally occupied with his business, which was on the verge of failing. He was almost never at home and, when at home, he was irritable and fatigued. John determined that his child's experience would be different. Consequently when the baby was born, John deliberately shared the activities of feeding and bathing the baby. He found, however, that his patience was frequently tried and he experienced emotions of anger toward the baby that were frightening. Without really being aware of the process, he began devising a series of chores and errands he "had" to do the moment the baby

needed attention. When his withdrawal from involvement with the baby was brought to his attention, he realized that he had been repeating his father's pattern without really knowing why.

The husband's relationship to his wife has to include their common child, who, though wanted, may still seem an intruder to them both. Theoretical ideas about how one wants to live and bring up children are put to the test, at first by anticipation, then by the real demands and needs of a real child and the parents' feelings toward the child.

Pregnancy presents special problems to the active, competent woman whose self-image is that of someone able to cope with, to master, and to stay in control of life situations. Pregnancy, while not an illness, usually involves seeing a physician, and this may be her first experience as a "patient" vulnerable to the symptoms, mood changes, and other unexpected physical and psychological experiences of the pregnant state. It may be disconcerting to her, as well as surprisingly gratifying, to feel herself identified with other women in such a widely shared experience. The opening up of new feelings and the new vulnerability to "symptoms" may eventually create in such a woman the potential for greater empathy with others, a quality often highly valued. As part of the shift in roles she may feel a sense of identification with and greater understanding of her mother. Even women who have had an abortion for an unwanted pregnancy sometimes remark that just the experience of being pregnant, albeit briefly, has made them more aware of their identity as a woman and left them with greater tolerance and empathy for other women.

The decision to work or to continue to work after the baby is born has a variety of motivations. There is one motivation for work by necessity and another for work by choice; and even if work is chosen, the motivation will differ, depending on whether a woman works primarily to earn money, to fill time, or to avoid the tensions and anxieties of staying home and satisfying the demands of small children. Such motivations contrast sharply with the free choice of working because of dedication to a career or the wish to develop her potential. Even a career-committed woman may be expressing a mixture of motives, and being "required" to work may serve to validate the decision for someone who is uncertain or conflicted. This may be particularly important to the woman who feels under pressure, either unconscious or conscious, to stay home and care for the child on a full-time basis. For the woman who has no choice about working, the decision may be easier but the inner conflict is no less unsettling. In fact, a rigid expectation in either direction creates problems for the woman.

A serious work commitment brings many complexities to the arrangements of family life for women (and men) in our society, which is not really prepared for this contingency. Priorities have to be set and reset, and decisions made and made again as to the importance of particular activities with children versus work commitments. Inventiveness and resourcefulness are important in resolving these complexities, but so are time, money, and support from others, to say nothing of the needed family models showing how such arrangements have been worked out without detriment to children or the marital relationship. In some instances pressure may have to be applied to change institutional regulations or policies. One personal requisite is the ability of both wife and husband to be flexible in modifying expectations of home and family.

Potentially there are many different solutions. Employing domestic help is one. For child care, help may be available in the form of a transient baby-sitter, or a live-in sitter who exchanges certain services for room and board, or, occasionally but not often, a full-time housekeeper. For housecleaning, a houseworker or cleaning service may be secured on a regular, periodic basis. In some localities there are "accommodaters," who will prepare a meal, serve it, and clean up afterwards. One of these services on a regular basis would provide time for other activities. Outside the home, day care centers have become more popular and more available, although generally they remain rather scarce.

To some extent the children themselves may be used as helpers more than they customarily are in middle-class families of comparable small size—much as they have been used in other cultures, where children of six or seven have been entrusted with the major care and supervision of a younger sibling in large families. One currently popular solution to the problem is a shift in the tasks shared by the husband. With the exception of breast-feeding there is virtually no household task that could not be performed by a man. Thus reorganization of household chores based on dual participation may free crucial hours for the woman who must meet the demands of an outside work schedule. Turning to a husband to share household tasks, however, presupposes that he is able and willing to share them. More is involved than the logistics of who does the cooking or the dishes or who cares for the baby at any given time. Important changes are involved in how the man and woman regard each other and relate to each other. He must give up some of his expectations that *his* supper will be prepared, *his* laundry done promptly, and so on.

The man may also feel threatened by the implication that if he allows himself to take part in domestic activities, he will no longer be "masculine." When his sense of masculinity is shaky or is dependent on the approval of other men, he may become upset if teased about his domestic role. Furthermore, caring activities demand patience and the overt expression of positive feelings, combined with the ability to integrate one's own wishes for gratification or achievement with responsiveness to the child's needs, which at any given moment may be urgent.

Traditionally these are all abilities associated with feminine qualities. Yet if men are to function effectively in similar roles, it will be necessary for them to develop the capacity for the integration of their own gratification with similar abilities. Moreover, household tasks will only be shared effectively when the husband has made a serious and sustained commitment to do so. The woman's problems will not be resolved if the husband "plays" at child care when he feels like it or does the dishes as "a favor" when he has no work of his own to do or when there is nothing interesting to watch on TV.

However, the crucial question that continues to concern the woman who goes to work while raising children is, what is the psychological effect of it all on the child? Most parents are deeply concerned with the development of the child, and most of them are aware of the psychological theory that the first years of the child's life are especially important in providing the basis for later healthy emotional development. This theory has been invoked to stress the importance of the mothering role, and has been interpreted by some to mean that a mother should devote herself full time to child care in the first few years. The recent attempts to refute this interpretation of the theory have stressed the quality of mothering rather than full-time motherhood, but without defining the characteristics of "quality" mothering. The fact is that no one really knows the key components of effective mothering or providing a "proper" maternal environment for the child. There is evidence to suggest that full-time attendance by the mother is not necessary, but no one has clear guidelines on what is necessary, although we know from clinical experience that a consistent relationship between the child and a primary adult is extremely important for the child's development.

Despite the lack of clear, scientific information about the effects on her child of a mother's working, our culture considers child care to be the responsibility of the mother. Thus, the woman who adopts a nontraditional pattern of family living is made to feel guilty by all kinds of people—neighbors, friends, husband, mother, mother-in-law, and children—who reproach her for leaving home. Guilt feelings are aroused that may reinforce internal unconscious feelings which are a residue from her own childhood development. A woman who genuinely feels it is important for a child to be able to separate from her when she does household errands will thoughtfully and carefully help the child to do so, secure in her conviction that she is being a good mother. The same mother, however, may feel highly ambivalent when the errands are replaced by a job, and she must leave the child at regular times. Those women who have had problems with separation in their own lives will feel particularly vulnerable as they identify with the child, sometimes inappropriately, and this may not in the long run be helpful to the child's development.

Another important unknown that bears directly on the question of sharing child care duties relates to the child's unconscious psychological identification. An attempt has already been made here to describe the complex manner in which a girl or a boy develops identification with female or male figures in the environment. There has been a strong presumption that these psychosexual identifications are fundamental to a sound sense of self and to adult functioning as a male or as a female, at least sexually. If mother and father divide all tasks equally, will the child have a clear-cut sense of two sexes simply from their anatomical differences? And if not, does it matter?

Cross-cultural studies suggest that every society makes relatively clear gender distinctions, but we do not really know what the effect on children would be if these distinctions were for all intents and purposes functionally blurred. It is tempting to suggest that parents should offer, first, a model of humanness and, secondarily but not inconsequentially, a model of secure gender identity, either male or female but one not bound to stereotyped gender roles. Unfortunately, it is not clear what meaning such a statement has, because, unless it involves some concept of differentiation between the sexes—that is, traits characteristic of one sex or the other—its meaning seems obscure.

Despite the burgeoning population control movement, social pressure for parenthood remains very strong. For a woman who genuinely wants to stay home with her children during their early years, it may be difficult to reenter a professional field some years later. This possibility faces her with a difficult choice. For a woman with a serious career interest, the conflict may be external as well as internal. The external problems of providing care for the children and the household are compounded by the structure of many work situations. Statement #7 by a woman Ph.D. notes some of these external difficulties:

> Child care was always an issue when the children were younger. I relied a lot on babysitters, and my kids still hold me to task for one really bad nursery school they were in. I owe my dissertation to one woman friend who did a lot of substitute mothering (they could then get by without sitters) while I put in an 18 hour day for a couple of months. I've always been fortunate in working with people who were most flexible about time off for getting kids to the doctor's, school conferences, and so on.
>
> Time for research in a medical school is difficult to come by *for anyone*. The primary demands are for clinical work and teaching; but promotion and tenure depend upon publication. The men who publish do so by putting in many hours after work. Recently I have been unwilling to put in that kind of "killer" schedule—at least until my children are gone, which won't be very many more years. By then, however, I may well have jeopardized my chances of promotion and tenure, which means termination.

In a given field, flexible work arrangements may be impossible and part-time work may accord lower status and be less interesting and rewarding than a full schedule. Moreover, the woman may be vulnerable to the accusation that she is not "a good mother." For a working mother this vulnerability is heightened and she is ready to feel guilty whenever anything "goes wrong." She may feel more strongly than the full-time mother that she has to do everything perfectly, which only adds to her tension and feelings of burden. The following quote from a paper written by a woman about the woman physician provides an example:

> To perform in a traditional medical career and carry out the activities of a traditional wife and mother is clearly impossible, and one has to develop alternative solutions and roles. In the past the availability of household help to the middle class or professional woman allowed for the possibility of greater independence. Current social patterns demand different life styles and a reconsideration of these traditional family roles so that a woman who becomes a physician does not have to be a "special" person who must essentially perform two or more full-time jobs.
>
> Women in medicine who also have families face the same problems as women with other serious work commitments and families. In addition to the demands of the profession, there are the complexities of functioning in a deviant way from the pattern in a particular community. It is easy to feel guilty if something doesn't go right at home—guilt which is reinforced by comments of sometimes hostile neighbors (who may be deeply envious). Even in a friendly environment some sense of conflict is potentially very close to the surface. "Am I doing the right thing?" is a latent question. Constant reassessments take place: weighing the value of a professional meeting, for instance, against the disruption of family patterns. Most of these issues are solvable; it is enormously helpful if there are others doing the same thing and pursuing similar solutions. Other women in medicine serving as role models offering peer support are immensely important.[7]

This is true in fields other than medicine. Furthermore, there is the "pull" of the mothering role which provides satisfactions that may interfere with career demands, as Statement #8 from a faculty woman indicates:

> Now that I've had a child I realize I wouldn't want to be away full-time from my family which, Women's Lib notwithstanding, has become a very important part of my life. This makes publications, so necessary for academic progress, much harder to produce, especially in science, which requires large blocks of time away from home. I'm not sure how I'll resolve this eventually.

Women not only need permission to find life styles that may differ from those of people who are important to them, but they need a diversity of other people who can serve as role models and teachers. This can be immensely helpful in validating the decision to adopt a certain life style and also in providing solutions for various practical problems with real-life illustrations of how they have been solved successfully. It is important likewise for men to have models of older women who have worked out solutions to such problems in nontraditional ways. A prominent woman sociologist suggested a kind of how-to-do-it handbook that would offer suggestions for coping with particular problems peculiar to the working mother. There are data indicating that a very important determinant of a woman's choice to work outside the home and to continue working after becoming a mother may be that her own mother worked and that her relationship with her mother was satisfactory.[8]

Where both prerequisites are fulfilled, the woman has an excellent and highly influential model. This is illustrated by a further quotation from the same woman Ph.D. quoted above (Statement #7):

> Important last thought—many women in my field have had enormous conflicts over the professional vs. female

issue, and I think it's been responsible for many giving up before reaching the degree. I had my share of that, but it was easier for several reasons: (1) I had made it as a wife and mother. (2) My own mother is an engineer and her example was very useful to me. (3) Despite my worst fears I continue to be confirmed as a woman (in the best sense of that word) by male friends and colleagues.

Obviously, many women will not have a mother who can be a role model in this respect, but some of them can find another older woman to serve as a substitute.

Later phases of child-rearing

Babies make special demands on their families; toddlers and older children make different ones. At each stage of the child's development the necessary parental adaptations will be different and they are constantly changing.[9] One of the earliest and most continuing needs of all children is for care while the mother or caretaking person is absent. It becomes increasingly difficult in modern life to find a housekeeper or nursemaid for this purpose. Day care facilities provide one answer, although only a partial one, and they are not widely available. In some families it is possible for the father to share equally in the care of the child and household duties. This may be only an expedient arrangement, or it may be a valuable method of shifting away from stereotypes of masculine and feminine roles, in which event it may contribute to more meaningful family relationships. At present, however, few fathers are able or are motivated to share equally in family tasks when this necessitates working part time.

Some working-class families have traditionally used this arrangement, not for ideological reasons but because the two parents work alternate shifts. But it is difficult to have a meaningful family life under such conditions, and the parents may rarely see each other. Those fathers who do share child

care are sometimes surprised and even a little guilty about
how much they enjoy it. And this sharing can lead to unexpected problems, such as the development of subtle competition between mother and father for the position of "best
mother." The woman who initially saw the process of sharing
primarily as a means of lightening her burdens may suddenly
find herself feeling threatened.

Many changes are being discussed and explored by young
couples today in efforts to devise alternative ways of organiz-
ing family life and child care. Alternative family role definitions permitting mother and father to share more equally in
the care of children are especially being sought. For example,
in areas with a predominance of young families, particularly
in middle-class neighborhoods with a large population of
academic and professional people, teachers schedule trips to
museums or other outings where fathers as well as mothers
come to help. When parents are asked to donate a day of their
time to a school project—a request which formerly brought a
response only from mothers—fathers may now appear. But it
is not yet clear how widespread these changes are.

As children grow older, the hours that must be devoted to
their actual care and supervision decrease. School attendance
and other activities take over the hours, but paradoxically
children may become more insistent on having a parent
rather than a babysitter available when they want or need an
adult. The child wants the particular qualities the parent has
to offer and is not mollified by the presence of a relatively
unknown person. Consequently, demands on the parents
may not diminish. One woman who seems to have worked out
a reasonably satisfactory solution is still concerned by this
problem:

> CASE VIGNETTE 10: Phyllis is a married, 31-year old medi-
> cal student who has two children. Her mother is a housewife
> whom she describes as strong, stubborn and a perfectionist

with whom she has a subservient relationship. Her father, who was brought up in an Eastern culture, has been entirely wrapped up in his business life without outside interests. She has very little in common with him on a day-to-day basis but she is proud of his praise and avoids his displeasure at almost any cost. Both parents have a high school education.

Because of her enjoyment of science in college Phyllis first thought of medicine as a career, and her parents' attitudes played an important part in the final choice. She states, "My father seemed to respect physicians so highly... I suppose I thought it would make me feel less subservient to my mother." Both parents encouraged this career choice. Her final decision was not made, however, until she married her physician husband. She felt that an important factor in the decision was having a husband who was willing to make the sacrifices necessary for her to continue her career. Furthermore, she had studies in other areas of medical science and found she was unhappy in a laboratory setting.

Medical school has not changed Phyllis' concept of herself as a woman; she still sees herself as a wife and mother first. She is concerned about the amount of time away from her children. "We have a good nurse and all I can do is hope that it will not be too detrimental. If it is, I will stop my career. But I feel quite certain that rather than my children suffering from my absence, it will be I who suffers because I will not see them as much as I would like." Going back to work part time shortly after delivery is not detrimental to the children, she feels. "I believe firmly that there are no bad consequences so long as the child knows the mother loves him and during the time she is home she gives him the attention and care he needs." She looks forward to her internship and a residency in her area of specialization.

In short, there seems to be no easy or uniform solution to the woman's problem of combining career and family. Various life and family patterns may be found which differentially fit the personalities, resolve the problems, and are appropriate to the relationships characterizing particular couples.

And for a given couple these patterns may change over time as one phase of marriage and family development succeeds another. Flexibility on the part of both partners and their refusal to accept rigid gender role stereotypes favor solution of their problems. A willingness to tolerate deviation from cultural expectations is also important if the partners are subjected, as they may well be, to hostility or criticism by friends or relatives. The ability to establish value priorities, to compromise, and to accept lowered standards in some areas also contributes significantly, especially where children claim attention. As parents they may want more time with their children and find themselves in conflict when outside work or necessary household chores interfere with purely recreational activities involving the children.

It is necessary to recognize that a couple cannot have total freedom of action for both members. If one member has total freedom, their relationship is that of master and servant, not a relationship of mutuality. Once this limitation is recognized, it may be possible to accept the fact that every couple living together will experience some conflict requiring compromise, and it has been questioned whether two people living together can be equally fulfilled. Presumably the arrangement will on balance provide more pleasure than pain, but it will inevitably involve some sharing of work that is either tedious or unpleasant. To be able to do this without feeling exploited or frustrated depends largely on the maturity of the partners and on the energy they invest in resolving the inevitable problems.

There are many pressures and temptations for a woman to give up working, or at least to declare a moratorium until the children are grown, and by this move to retreat from the complexities of combining career and family. The cultural option to leave a career is often greater and more acceptable for a woman than a man unless economic or psychological necessity requires her to work. Tartakoff refers to the "regressive pull of motherhood," noting that such shifts, which may have started in pregnancy, are often continued after childbirth.[10] In fact, any disruption of the balance of the woman's life, such as difficulties in making child care or housekeeping arrangements, the demands of the husband's career, or the need to move geographically may serve as a stimulus to give up her career. Another temptation "to stop" derives from the competitive nature of many professional or business work situations. For a woman it is possible to stay home, care for her children, and avoid the conflicts of the marketplace while leading a life that is approved by convention. For many women this will be the adaptive, preferred choice, and one that should not be deprecated. It may, however, reflect a retreat from conflict, and this aspect is stressed because so many factors press toward giving up outside work.

Men as well as women may be disturbed by the pressures and anxieties indigenous to career and work or may experience problems with achievement and success, but in our society men live with the opposite cultural expectations, which are equally limiting. They cannot avoid competitive strains without running the risk of significantly diminishing themselves in their own eyes or in the eyes of those around them. Up until now, however, they have not had much responsibility in the domestic sphere, so that while their obligations may have been difficult to meet, they have not had to oppose traditional expectations in order to meet them. Finally, the needs of the child must be considered in any family arrangement: The complete equation for the satisfactory distribution of family responsibilities must balance the needs, gratifications and capacities of all three—mother, father and child.

REFERENCES

1. Group for the Advancement of Psychiatry. CONSIDERATIONS OF PERSONALITY DEVELOPMENT IN COLLEGE STUDENTS, Report No. 32 (New York: GAP, 1955).
2. Matina Horner. Fail: Bright Women, *Psychology Today* 3 (1969): 36.

3. David Tresemer. Fear of Success: Popular, but Unproven. *Psychology Today*, 7, 10 (1974); 82-85.
4. Lois W. Hoffman. Early Childhood Experiences and Women's Achievement Motives, *Journal of Social Issues* 28 (1972): 129-155.
5. Matina Horner. Toward an Understanding of Achievement-Related Conflicts in Women, *Journal of Social Issues* 28 (1972): 157-175.
6. Lois W. Hoffman. Fear of Success in Males and Females: 1965 and 1972, *Journal of Consulting & Clinical Psychology*, in press.
7. Carol Nadelson & Malkah T. Notman. The Woman Physician, *Journal of Medical Education* 47 (1972): 176-183.
8. Grace K. Baruch. Maternal Influences upon College Women's Attitudes toward Women and Work, *Developmental Psychology* 6 (1972): 32-37.
9. James Anthony & Therese Benedek. PARENTHOOD: ITS PSYCHOLOGY AND PSYCHOPATHOLOGY (Boston: Little, Brown, 1970).
10. Helen H. Tartakoff. "Psychoanalytic Perspectives on Women: Past, Present, and Future," prepared for the Conference, "Women: Resource for a Changing World," Radcliffe Institute, April 1972, Radcliffe College, Cambridge, Mass. 02138.

6

PSYCHOTHERAPY AND PSYCHOTHERAPISTS

Although formal psychotherapy* will only be experienced by a small percentage of college women, it is appropriate in a report by psychiatrists addressing the problems of the educated woman to discuss the impact of psychotherapy on women. Two facts must be recognized immediately: (1) that the majority of psychotherapists, on college campuses and off, have been male; and (2) that psychotherapy, though often striving for neutrality or a nondirective approach, does have an implicit value system. The latter fact may be denied or disguised, and the therapist's values may frequently be difficult or impossible to define precisely—nevertheless they exist.

As already noted, Freud's work has markedly influenced psychiatry and psychology in this country, and advertently or inadvertently, some of his views have helped to shape prevailing definitions of femininity as well as to imply certain "normative states" fundamental to the mental health of women, their maturation, fulfillment, or adaptation. A recent study by Inge Broverman and her colleagues suggests that many clinicians today view their female patients in much the same way Freud viewed his many years ago.[1] Broverman tested 79 therapists (46 male and 33 female psychiatrists, psychologists, and social workers) using a sex-role stereotype questionnaire.

---

* It is recognized that the term *psychotherapy* currently signifies a wide range of approaches and therapies. In this discussion, *psychotherapy* refers primarily to a psychoanalytically oriented, nondirective therapy, utilizing a modified technique of free association, in which an attempt is made to uncover certain unconscious feelings and to trace patterns of reaction with the aim of achieving psychological insight for the patient.

213

This test was comprised of 122 pairs of traits in apposition —for example, *very subjective . . . very objective; not at all aggressive . . . very aggressive.*

Investigators asked the subjects to rate each of these traits on a scale from 1 to 7 in terms of where a healthy male should fall, a healthy female, or a healthy adult (sex unspecified). They found that

a) There was close agreement among these clinicians on the attributes they felt characterized men, women and adults.

b) There were no major differences between the opinions of male and female clinicians.

c) Clinicians had standards of mental health for men that differed from those for women. Their standards for "healthy adult man" corresponded to those for "healthy adult"; but those for "healthy woman" differed from both by including submissiveness, emotionality, susceptibility to influence, sensitivity to hurts, excitability, conceit about their appearance, and dependency, coupled with a lack of adventurousness, competitiveness, aggressiveness and objectivity.

At the very least these findings suggest that clinicians, be they male or female, are influenced by stereotypes of women and men, which they share consciously. Although this study needs replication and the specific group of respondent therapists is not described, these findings cannot be ignored. And it is difficult to imagine that the stereotypes held do not influence the course of psychotherapy by these therapists.

One may ask how these stereotypes, or values based on such stereotypes, are transmitted from therapist to patient in the course of psychotherapy, and more particularly in a therapy which is nondirective. The answer is not clear-cut, but probably the route of transmission may be found in the interpretations of the therapist or the statements of the patient chosen by the therapist for exploration.[2] As noted in the foregoing, individuals make choices for a variety of reasons which in a psychodynamic framework can be thought of as adaptive or defensive (although probably most choices represent a combination of both). Most psychotherapists would take the position that a choice made primarily for defensive reasons was less constructive, more likely to prove unsatisfactory in the long run, and perhaps even pathological, compared to one made for adaptive reasons. To oversimplify for the moment, a woman may opt for marriage and motherhood, that is, for the more traditional female role. This may be a positive choice and if the therapist sees it as such, it will not be challenged. Certainly this role gratifies very real needs for creativity, dependency and passivity.

However, where the therapist feels that the choice is being made because the woman is anxious about pursuing a career or frightened of success, initiative, competition or independence, the choice may be questioned. The more likely to be questioned is the reverse choice, the choice against marriage and/or motherhood. The therapist who feels that total fulfillment for a woman requires these experiences probably will look on the choice as a defensive one and may strongly question the patient's underlying feelings, which in turn may lead the patient to reconsider and perhaps change her mind.

Or in the college setting, should a woman student elect to major in engineering, and, in exploring the reasons for her choice, the therapist focuses on the fact that her father is an engineer, questions may be raised about her "masculine" identification. But let us suppose that the father is a child psychiatrist and the woman chooses a major in child study. This choice might be accepted without question or comment by the therapist, who unconsciously feels it is an appropriate choice. Presumably, if the issue of masculine identification because the patient chose a career like that of the father is reasonable to explore in the first instance, it is equally reasonable in the second. Needless to say, these simplifications of a very complex process are not examples of approved psychotherapeutic technique, but rather attempts to show how a therapist's unconscious (and sometimes conscious) values may be transmitted to a patient.

It should be noted that any college student, male or female, who is attempting a redefinition of gender role does so within that student's developmental context. Thus, what may be "liberated" or "individuated" for a college freshman may be quite inappropriate for a college senior. Although this fact should be self-evident, it is not always considered by either students or therapists. Nevertheless, in a very real sense, explorations in identity definition should never be viewed as closed, and it is to be hoped, even desired, that they be viewed as a lifelong process, particularly within the context of the interpersonal relationship between a man and a woman. Such explorations continue as they define their roles in living together, marriage, work, the continuation of their education (who works while who goes to school), deciding whether or not to have children, how many to have, and how they should be raised (within the home or with the help of ancillary facilities, such as day care centers). This sense of openness about gender role definition should be a vital value for therapists in consultation just as we have suggested it should be for parents in child-rearing. Settling for the old stereotyped styles of raising a "real" boy or a "real" girl is certainly more comfortable, but it seems to perpetuate many of the values that lead to later difficulties with gender role.

A discussion of these concerns is not to suggest, as some women recently have suggested, that psychotherapy is no longer a viable source of help for women. What it does suggest is that therapists should reexamine some of their own values. More particularly, they must learn to recognize the stereotypes about gender role they hold consciously or unconsciously, must become more sensitive to unconscious influences shaping their own values, must struggle to eliminate the power strategies sometimes at play in therapy, or at least be aware how these limiting factors may be inadvertently introduced into therapy. Having gone through this evaluative process (and many experienced therapists have already done so), any therapist will be better able to help women and men redefine their gender roles, explore their options shared as human beings, and attain greater individuation and autonomy. In fact, the members of this committee believe that psychotherapy and psychoanalysis, although of limited availability, are, when freed from the burden of stereotypes, useful ways of clarifying unconscious determinants that bear on the manifest problem of gender role, and of removing some of the internal barriers that interfere with women's utilization of their full capacities.

REFERENCES

1. Inge K. Broverman, Susan Raymond Vogel, Donald M. Broverman, F. E. Clarkson & Paul S. Rosenkrantz. Sex-Role Stereotypes: A Current Appraisal, *Journal of Social Issues* 28 (1972): 59-78.
2. Joy K. Rice & David C. Rice. Implications of the Women's Liberation Movement for Psychotherapy, *American Journal of Psychiatry* 130 (1973): 191-196.

7

TOWARD CHANGE

Changes in women's roles

Some women will begin to challenge one or more aspects of the stereotyped gender roles in themselves and perhaps secondarily in men. They may do this for internal reasons, perhaps through positive identification with an older woman who works; or for more external reasons—perhaps because of an academic course on women's roles they may have taken, or the influence on their thinking of one of the Women's Liberation groups; or because of new demands made on them by divorce or widowhood. As they take up the challenge, the outcome will inevitably influence their interpersonal relationships. Some of these interpersonal consequences of a woman's redefinition of her gender role in relation to herself, other women, and men call for exploration here.

1—The woman's relationship to herself. The social position of women makes it difficult for them to achieve self-esteem. Saenger writes,

> The existence of a sound self-esteem which, in large measure, depends upon successful identification with one's group is fundamental for the development of well-adjusted personality. The feeling of being accepted, and accepting one's group, is basic for the individual's security. Where the group is considered inferior by the larger society, and membership in it related to deprivations, a positive identification with the group and the development of strong ties of belonging becomes difficult.[1]

Saenger believes that the minority group tends to accept the beliefs of the dominant group, which leads to feelings of ambiguity about the inferior role imposed and to a lack of self-worth resulting from the acceptance of these beliefs. *Even in individuals who do not accept these negative beliefs, the impact of prejudice and discrimination lowers self-esteem and heightens insecurity.*

As a result of two studies, McKee and Sherriffs concluded that college "men and women esteem men significantly more highly than women"[2] and that:

> ...men were considered frank and straightforward in social relations, intellectually rational and competent, and bold and effective in dealing with the environment. Men's undesirable characteristics are largely limited to excesses of these traits. The stereotype of women embraces the social amenities, emotional warmth, and a concern for affairs besides the material. In addition, women are regarded as guilty of snobbery and irrational and unpleasant emotionality. Male subjects particularly emphasized men's desirable characteristics; females emphasized women's neuroticism.[3]

Keniston and others have studied women who are trying to change and redefine their sex role through greater individuation, autonomy, and independence. He points out that these women justly complain of having no models for what they are trying to do.[4] Rossi has noted that it is acceptable for such women to admit ambivalent feelings toward roles which are optional, such as whether or not to enter a career.[5] The more critical the role for the (supposed) maintenance and survival of society, the greater the likelihood that the negative component of her ambivalence will be repressed by the woman and that unconscious barriers will be erected against its expression. Steinmann *et al* studied 75 college women, who appeared to perceive themselves and their "ideal woman" as essentially alike, with equal components of passive and active orientation; but they perceived man's "ideal woman" as significantly more passive and accepting of a subordinate role with respect to both their personality development and their place in family structure.[6]

It seems fair to say that an initial and critical task for a woman who wishes to respect herself as a whole person, and thus seriously consider her options in regard to career and/or marriage and children, involves three steps: (a) to identify with a competent older woman or family member who treats her aspirations seriously; (b) to respect and identify with women in her peer groups who are similarly self-involved; and (c) to work out a satisfactory relationship with a man who also takes her aspirations seriously, and who respects and encourages her intellect, activity, and competitiveness without being threatened. The significant man may be a boyfriend but he could just as well be a male faculty member, a therapist, or a counselor.

2—Relationship to other women. Keniston found in one study that women in the process of redefining their gender role assume that other women will probably make indifferent, boring or inferior companions.[7]

> Only prolonged exposure to another woman who is obviously not any of these things could alter this presumption. With men, however, the presumption was generally favorable: Men were expected to be lively and interesting; men's conversation was about more serious topics; time spent with men was usually better spent than time spent with women.

Keniston feels that it would be a mistake to look upon these women as depreciating women as such, but rather more correct to see them as "having sharply differentiated themselves from the majority of women and as assuming—perhaps correctly—that most women have not followed their pathway to development."[8]

Although Keniston's subjects may not be typical, it is not surprising that a number of women might share their attitudes, given some of the prevailing cultural stereotypes about women. In their work, the women he studied found that most of their colleagues were male, and that in their private lives they were involved in confirming and consolidating their new relationships with men.

> Only in special groups like Women's Liberation consciousness-raising groups does intimate contact with other women occur. When it does, some of the attitudes mentioned—e.g., the ambivalence and rejection of other women—tend to become more conscious and to be at least partly resolved. And only under these rather special circumstances are such young women likely to discover their deep bonds with each other.[9]

One aspect of women's relationship to each other that cannot be overlooked is the sexual. It is certainly conceivable that increased emphasis on the personal worth of women would lead to increased possibilities for homosexual attachments, both emotional and physical. In fact, lesbianism has been an issue in some of the groups within the women's movement, but it is quite impossible to ascertain whether there has been real increase in such relationships or whether they are simply more openly discussed in accord with the general openness of the Gay Liberation movement. If such relationships have become more common, this would not be surprising, in view of the current sentiment against further population expansion, the new approval of individual self-expression, and the stated opinion of some women that heterosexual marriage is a trap devised by men for their own benefit. Because a few of the more prominent feminists have made public statements about their own homosexual or bisexual orientation, there has been considerable publicity on the subject, but it is as yet unclear how significant such behavior will be for the average woman.

3—Relationships with men. Just as women who redefine their gender roles will need other women like themselves with whom they can relate comfortably, so they will need men who are willing to question the stereotypes of the masculine role. The task of finding a man who is willing to reexamine some of his own traditional, independent aggressiveness and competitiveness, perhaps forego some of it and allow the expression of similar qualities in a woman, is surely one of the major tasks of the woman seeking autonomy. But perhaps there is hope. In another study, Steinmann *et al* administered the same inventory of feminine values used in the study outlined above to 562 American college men.[10] Data from their questionnaires indicate that their "ideal woman" was significantly more active and self-assertive than the ideal which the women of the earlier Steinmann study attributed to them. These studies were conducted in 1964 and 1966, and there is more recent impressionistic evidence that college men and women to an increasing extent are getting closer to and becoming more aware of mutual areas of change and respect.

Insofar as a woman's career aspirations place her in competition with men, there seems to be less change. Horner notes evidence that even today highly intelligent women continue

> consciously or unconsciously [to] equate intellectual achievement with loss of femininity. A bright woman is caught in a double bind. In testing and other achievement-oriented situations she worries not only about failure but also about success. If she fails, she is not living up to her own standards of performance; if she succeeds, she is not living up to societal expectations about the female role. Men in our society do not experience this kind of ambivalence because they are not only permitted, but actively encouraged to do well. For women, then, the desire to achieve is often contaminated by the motive to avoid success.[11]

In Horner's test results, over 65 percent of the women, but fewer than 10 percent of the men showed evidence of "the motive to avoid success.... These findings suggest that most women will fully explore their intellectual potential only when they do not need to compete—and least of all, when they *are* competing with men."[12] One wonders if these women might not do better in an all-women college. If so, one would then have to ask whether they might not have to meet the problem later on.

> This was most true of women with a strong anxiety about success. Unfortunately, these are often the same women who could be very successful if they were free from that anxiety. The girls in [the] sample who feared success also tended to have high intellectual ability and histories of academic success. (It is interesting to note that all but two of these girls were majoring in the humanities and in spite of very high grade points, aspired to traditional female careers: housewife, mother, nurse, schoolteacher. Girls who did not fear success, however, were aspiring to graduate degrees and careers in such scientific areas as math, physics, and chemistry.)
>
> We can see from this small study that achievement-motivation in women is much more complex than is the same drive in men. Most men do not find many inhibiting forces in their path if they are able and motivated to succeed. As a result, they are not threatened by competition; in fact, surpassing an opponent is a source of pride and enhanced masculinity.
>
> In recent years many legal and educational barriers to female achievement have been removed; but it is clear that a psychological barrier remains. The motive to avoid success has an all too important influence on the intellectual and professional lives of women in our society.[13]

It is significant that "success" in this study was automatically assumed to be congruent with traditional masculine definitions of achievement.

Faced with these feelings about the consequences of academic or career success, women students deal in a variety

of ways with the issue of achievement in an intellectually
competitive field. Some attempt to be "better men" and to
perform as "one of the boys." Others unconsciously deny any
difficulties, fail to perceive negative attitudes, and learn to
appear passive, compliant, and uncompetitive. Still others
create an image of confusion, of being scatterbrained, either
deliberately as a cover-up, or inadvertently as a result of
conflicting internal self-images. A woman may feel that she
has to choose between a "feminine" style, usually somewhat
vague and scatterbrained, and one which is termed aggressive
and "castrating."

Any career-oriented woman may have more than one dis-
appointment in her search for men who can be flexible toward
her career plans and her self concept. She may begin to
wonder whether the end is worth the pain and loneliness
experienced in the process of reaching her goal. Keniston has
found a high tolerance for feelings of ambiguity and uncertainty in women who, while building a career, continue to try
to work out some nontraditional relationship with a man or
are willing to accept the risk that no such relationship will ever
materialize. He suggests that the capacity to endure this uncertainty may be a major factor in a woman's ability to stick to a
career path.

No such dilemma exists for the man. For him a career is
seen as a logical step preceding establishment of a permanent
relationship with a woman, although the sequence may at
times be changed. Conversely, for a woman, a career may be
seen as an unnecessary step which can complicate or prevent
establishment of a permanent relationship with a man and the
development of a family. Both goals remain important despite recent changes in attitude among college women suggesting that a career is considered equally important.[14]
Clearly these continuing disparities interfere with possibilities
for new modifications in male-female relationships.

Changes in men's roles

Thus far discussion has revolved almost exclusively about women, although much that has been said applies to men as well. The Committee has concerned itself with women because women have been the more neglected in our institutions of higher learning, which on the whole have acted as though there was only one sex in college. But from the viewpoint of male development and the relations between men and women, men have been constrained in their own way. As with women, models for changed male roles are not readily available. To give up the stereotype of independent, aggressive competitiveness without being deprecated as "feminine" by oneself, other men, women, or society in general is an issue that confronts men just as exquisitely as comparable issues confront women.

The price men appear to have paid for following the stereotypes of competitiveness and aggressiveness, along with their concomitant goals of success and achievement, has been high. The evidence accumulated by psychosomatic medicine points to the fact that many forms of psychosomatic illness, regardless of causative factors, occur more frequently in men than in women, particularly in men who are found to be unaccepting of their own dependency needs. Similarly, there is a much higher prevalence in men of cardiovascular disease such as stroke, coronary occlusion, and hypertension. In part, current theory relates this to the emotional component in men that associates hostile, hard-driving qualities with the maintenance of a satisfactory masculine self-image. It remains to be seen whether role changes currently in progress will affect the incidence and age of onset of such illnesses in women.

There are other indications of important changes. In a recent study of college students,[15] male respondents were supportive of women's strong orientation toward having a career for the sake of their own development. Furthermore, men are now generally more willing to accept the idea that women will share in providing for the economic needs of the family, even though many but by no means all men continue to see themselves as the primary breadwinner. Finally, over 60 percent of both men and women students in the study cited agreed that their participation in child-rearing tasks should be about equal. It appears that some men are beginning to visualize a greater participation in tasks previously considered feminine, and presumably when family tasks are more evenly divided, the rat race of business or professional life may become less than all-engulfing.

As men change the concept of their gender role, they may also look for women with qualities and goals that are different from those traditionally thought of as desirable. It should be remembered, however, that it is easier to express such attitudes verbally than it is to carry them out in actual practice. It is difficult to anticipate one's reactions when actually faced with the demands of family.

Changes in marital relationships

The relatively new concept of the "egalitarian marriage," which is related to that of the dual-career family, is a natural outgrowth of the movement for equality for women. In the past, marriage has been based on a concept of complementarity, with husband and wife filling clear-cut roles in the marital relationship. These roles varied in different societies and in different social groups within a society, and although practice often deviated from theory, the cultural ideal was unmistakable. Depending on social class and particular viewpoint, there were differences of opinion as to who had the best of the bargain, but there was no question that it was a bargain in the trading sense of the word. Neither partner was expected to stray very far from the agreed-upon roles. Generally, in our society, the woman was responsible for food preparation,

child care, home care, and the selection of household fixtures
and clothing; the man was responsible for earning money, the
heavy home tasks, the purchase of major house items, and
often family "business" matters. Over the years, however, this
model has been questioned, and the recent feminist movement has strongly protested the concept and its consequences.
If the educated woman is going to have the opportunity to use
her training in any sort of career, modifications are essential.

The alternate suggestion is the egalitarian marriage, which
postulates equal opportunity for each partner and an adaptation that does not consign either partner automatically to a
particular role or task within the marital framework. This is a
laudable ideal, but one that in practice clearly requires considerable ingenuity, flexibility, and goodwill on the part of both
partners if it is to work. For any two people living together
there is a minimum of tasks that must be completed in order to
facilitate the business of living, and with a child or children
added, this minimum significantly increases and the tasks
themselves become more complex.

The area in which equality can be established most unequivocally is the area of outside occupation. When both partners have a career, however, it is possible to visualize situations
in which the interests of one might come into conflict with the
interests of the other. Recently several researchers, notably
the Rapoports[16] and Holmstrom,[17] have studied the two-
career family and have drawn some conclusions as to how
couples have satisfactorily worked out the problems involved.
In a study on couples with children, the Rapoports conclude
that the essential adaptation is "a division of labour in relation
to family functions that is distributed between the partners on
an equal-style basis." Thus, various household and family
support tasks were divided by "skills and inclinations present
in the specific partnership" rather than by traditional gender
role determinations. All couples, however, were dependent
on the availability of some domestic help and had to assign

priorities for child care, house care, and leisure and social activities.

Some of the couples studied were inclined to choose, when possible, jobs that did not "spill over" into nonworking periods, and they stressed the importance of a rather careful organization of necessary tasks so that the more important tasks (i.e., child care) would not be neglected as a result of time consumed by less significant activities. The Rapoports also observed lines of tension between partners which were handled in a variety of ways by different couples. Sometimes a partner (more often the wife) adopted a different "personality," one at work and one at home; in some cases a clear-cut opportunity for one partner was sacrificed because there was no acceptable concomitant opportunity for the other; and there were transient periods for some couples when one partner shouldered more of the household activities than the other.

The Rapoports developed a cost-benefit scheme of evaluation and applied it to five technically defined dimensions of stress.[18] In general, couples seemed to work out solutions by establishing lines of demarcation about all activities within which they felt they could comfortably function as separate and distinct individuals. At times it was necessary to work out efficiency procedures which were at odds with normative customs prevailing. This sometimes resulted in guilt feelings for the individual and often led to resentment and criticism from friends and relatives—a consequence which presumably will ensue less and less often as the dual-career family becomes more prevalent. The investigators point out that different periods within the marriage may place peak strain on one or another aspect of family functioning, and it is their opinion that accommodation to this phenomenon is essential to family balance. They stress the need for flexibility on the part of both the partners *and* the society.

In a similar study, Holmstrom described four barriers to

success of the dual-career marriage: (1) the pressure to move geographically for career advancement; (2) the definition of career as an all-consuming activity; (3) the concept of the wife as an auxiliary aide to the husband's career (e.g., as hostess); and (4) the difficulty of raising children in the isolated nuclear family.[19] In her study, the issue of geography arose among 75 percent of the respondent couples and in every case the wife's career has been affected by the husband's move. Surprisingly, in many cases the wife's career also affected at least once the decision where to live, although the husband remained the determining factor in family relocation significantly more often than the wife. With regard to the other three barriers, concerted effort and often considerable adaptation were required to overcome them. For example, time became a particularly scarce commodity and highly efficient schedules had to be devised for both partners. Holmstrom feels that society should make greater adaptations to help solve the problems she found among these couples.

Rosenkrantz conducted a study on egalitarian families and found as an immediate difficulty the lack of suitable models.[20] He also concluded that when the family has children, gender role conflicts were much more in evidence because "there is just much more work when children arrive." One characteristic of the couples he studied was a more open display of and tolerance for conflict. He found, on the other hand, that the working through of these conflicts, where successful, seemed to strengthen the union. He found that the couples studied placed a high value on intimacy, and he points out that dependency behavior is not eliminated but rather transformed into greater adaptability, that is, "a more flexible choice of appropriate ways of expressing...dependency needs, of differentiating appropriate circumstances and appropriate people on whom to be dependent."

Children put a particular strain on this marital model and, whether in response to some anticipation of this problem or as a result of increasing awareness of the need for population control, more individuals currently are contemplating marriage without children. A recent study indicated that 10 to 15 percent of students polled did not want children. Since the Depression and until very recently, the pressure to procreate has been very strong, and it is safe to say that most couples married during this period with the expectation that they would have at least one child. It is difficult to know how many of those who did not have children remained childless out of choice, but their number is probably relatively small. With the development of satisfactory, reasonably foolproof methods of contraception, the choice not to reproduce is now open to every couple, and simultaneously efforts toward population control have for the first time placed a positive social value on nonprocreation. Thus, a couple may find it possible today to consider their own feelings about having a child and make a deliberate decision against doing so. This unquestionably lightens the burdens of family maintenance and lessens the conflicts between career and home responsibilities. It may in particular decrease demands on the woman and minimize the sharp conflict between child care responsibilities during the early years and heavy work obligations at a crucial period in the establishment of her career. As with so many choices, however, the decision may be determined more by unconscious feelings than by conscious planning.

Even if children are desired by the dual-career couple, limiting the number and spacing their arrival may reduce the time and energy necessary for child care at any given period. At one time the one-child family was considered a less than ideal environment for the child, but recent studies seem to have disproved this belief. Many families now feel that two children is the ideal number, when a generation ago four or five were frequently desired and produced. But it should not be forgotten that there are many unconscious gratifications satisfied by having a family and that the current rationale for small families may be superseded by another rationale which reverses the trend.

The concept of equality in marriage has been an important new development in the United States, but it is still so novel that it is difficult to do more than cite the problems encountered and the empirical solutions so far attempted. In any event, the dual-career family calls for considerable flexibility on the part of the partners, whose adjustment could be greatly aided by greater flexibility on the part of society.

Changes in living patterns

Some possible changes in permanent patterns of living have been touched on. Currently, however, more revolutionary breaks with past living arrangements have been proposed, among which are "open marriage," communal living, homosexual marriage, and the single state.

1—Open marriage. This concept in a certain sense embodies an attempt to respond to the increase in human longevity and the great reduction in time that must be devoted to child-rearing. Marriage today may have several distinct phases during which the needs of the partners change significantly. As defined by the O'Neills, open marriage involves an open attitude to the relationship which revises many of the standard conventions.[21] For the O'Neills, this does not imply extramarital sexual relationships, although they are not ruled out. It presumably allows the woman greater flexibility in the pursuit of a career because it diminishes the expectation that each partner will carry out preordained roles. Thus, issues like separation of the partners that may be required by career, or transitory relations with others, are to be seen as part of the expectable pattern of the marriage rather than as evidence of marital tension. How well this concept of marriage will work in practice is not as yet clear.

2—Communal living. This has been a rather conspicuous pattern of living in the past few years. In many communes, the group is held together by common interests or by one guiding principle, such as a set of religious beliefs or a rejection of urban living and an active commitment to farm life. Theoretically, the communal living situation reincarnates the living situation of the extended family in the period preceding World War I, although factually this was never the cultural or statistical norm of living in American society. It envisions a sharing of child-rearing tasks and housekeeping chores that allows a woman with a baby to work outside the home relieved of the need to make elaborate and often unreliable baby-sitting arrangements. Furthermore, theoretically the existence of "multiple mothers" may decrease the dependence of the child on the biological mother, thus minimizing the influence of a prolonged exclusive relationship between child and mother, and the possible psychological harm the child might suffer by the absence of the only mother figure. The Kibbutz of Israel, although initially developed from a somewhat different motivation, has unquestionably provided an influential model, accounting to some extent for the current popularity of communal living concepts in this country.

3—Homosexual marriage. Although this arrangement has probably had an informal and clandestine existence for some time, it has only recently emerged as an alternate living arrangement. Its public debut on the current social horizon is in part related to the recent emergence of the Gay Liberation movement, which, in addition to protesting general social discrimination against homosexually oriented individuals, has called attention to the inequities of tax laws, adoption laws, and some housing codes. The concept of homosexual marriage has appealed to those women who feel that true independence for them means the exclusion of men from their significant relationships. Obviously, homosexual marriages pose the same potential problems of dominance, division of labor, priority of careers and so on as heterosexual marriages. Nevertheless some women feel that these problems become very different when stereotypes of male and female gender roles are not involved and the weight of tradition does not burden the relationship with guilt or resentment.

4—The single state. Not all women in the past have married, although one might deduce from reading about single women that those who have remained single have not done so out of choice. Actually, there is some evidence to suggest that women in the earlier part of the century who elected to pursue serious careers at least harbored a subliminal awareness and acceptance of the possibility that they might not marry. What is not clear is whether they elected to remain single in order to be able to continue with their work; whether they saw marriage and career as incompatible, and, perhaps reluctantly, chose the latter; whether their competence made them frightening to men, so that relationships with men did not develop; or whether their earning power made it unnecessary for them to accept a less-than-ideal proposal of marriage merely to guarantee economic security for themselves.

Parenthetically, it should be noted that many women developed significant careers after becoming widows, suggesting that at least in the past the single state was combined more often than marriage with a career. In any event, given the social mores of the period, the single state essentially meant giving up interpersonal sexual activity. Some women may have managed liaisons, but these arrangements obviously had hazards in the social climate of the times and rarely could be acknowledged openly. Today, however, with a more permissive attitude toward sexual activity outside marriage, a woman can elect to remain single and still maintain an active sexual life. She can even bear (or with some difficulty adopt) and raise a child without evoking the social opprobrium that would have greeted her even a generation ago. For some women unmarried motherhood has attractions because it sidesteps conflicts over job priorities, geographic location of the family, and even the necessity for establishing marital division of labor, but it exacerbates the demands of child care because there is no husband with whom to share the responsibility.

It is too soon to asses the long-range effects of any of these patterns for living. It is possible to see advantages and disadvantages in all of them and it is safe to say that not everyone could or would be able to adapt to each pattern. Furthermore, it would be naive to assume that these patterns are totally acceptable today any more than they would have been a decade ago. In fact, there is considerable evidence that many adults continue to disapprove of homosexual behavior and of both premarital and extramarital sexual activity, so that a woman electing one or another of these patterns still may expect to meet with social disapproval.[22] It should be noted, however, that in one study on campus only 10 percent of college students disapproved of premarital sex, which would indicate either that attitudes are changing or that younger population groups have values significantly different from their elders.[23]

Probably the main benefit to be gained from a scrutiny of these patterns is that they challenge many of our unconsciously held assumptions, and this may serve to hold a mirror to more conventional living patterns. If the homosexual pair can work out harmonious patterns of joint living that do not automatically make assumptions about gender role or dominance and submission, it is only logical to ask why a heterosexual pair cannot do the same. Indeed, recognition of the very existence of different living patterns stresses that the needs and preferences of people differ and that resistance to conformity should be encouraged rather than condemned.

Changes in institutions

Allusions have been made to the need for and the possibility of changes in institutional patterns. It is not easy to forecast all of these and it is clear that some of them can only take place gradually over a period of time. Thus, the importance of models for women college students has been suggested, but it will take time before women in large numbers will be available as candidates for faculty, business, and professional positions because at the moment only a relatively few women have gone through the necessary preparatory steps.[24] It is important for this reason that the women presently prepared for and interested in such posts be helped by institutions rather than blocked by rigid institutional policies that were designed for different purposes in an era now past.

One example of such policies is the so-called nepotism policy that existed (or exists) in many colleges. Actually this is usually an "anti-nepotism" regulation that prohibits the employment of both husband and wife by the college or department within the college. It is doubtful that the original purpose of this policy was to prevent women from progressing in careers. Presumably it was designed to prevent the possibility of special privilege accruing to one member of the couple as a result of influence by the other and to avoid situations in which action taken in relation to one partner might create difficulty or embarrassment for the spouse. In effect, however, it has operated to prevent both partners of a couple from working in perhaps the only appropriate jobs available in a given geographical area. Inasmuch as the man's career usually has been the determining factor in the choice of family location, the operation of a "nepotism policy" meant that the woman was forced to travel long distances for a suitable job, work at a job on a lower level, or give up all pretense to a career. For such reasons, elimination of "nepotism policies" where they still exist is an indicated change clearly called for.

Other overdue institutional changes concern the need for greater flexibility in leave policies, more part-time opportunities, and work schedules that consider the child care responsibilities of qualified candidates. Frequently these are not easy to work out, but institutions committed to the larger

policy of encouraging women to assume a more realistic share
of the job opportunities available must give the same careful
thought to the enforcement of these changes that a commercial enterprise gives to improving its profit margins. There is a
longstanding tradition in many institutions granting employees a certain number of sick leave days a year. This practice
could be extended to apply to sick care by the employee for
others. Even though working women with children probably
do take time off to care for a sick child, they should be able to
do so without feeling that they are doing something unto-
ward. If a similar policy were established for men, care of the
sick could be shared and the issue of who in the family was sick
would be less important than that care was provided in answer
to an employee's genuine need.

Maternity and paternity leave is a conspicuous example of
an important change that has been effected in their personnel
policy by some organizations. The use of part-time employees
is another. In the latter situation, institutions should probably
do more than simply permit part-time work or study. One of
the problems of part-time employment is that the part-time
worker so often feels isolated from the mainstream of activities, more of a "piece worker" than anything else. Institutions might recognize this as a problem and attempt to relate
their part-time workers to the functioning of the total organization. One suggested method adapts the "partnership principle" whereby a given job (suited to such treatment) is split
between two workers, who share the responsibility for information exchange much as nurses or doctors pass on orders
and reports of the outgoing shift to the incoming shift.

Child care poses particularly difficult problems for a variety
of reasons, but it could use new solutions. Some of the problems have to do with the conflict already noted—that is, between the peak demand for child care, which occurs early in
most people's careers and a concurrent demand for especially
hard work in the process of establishing oneself in one's cho-

sen field. Day care is frequently suggested as an answer. This may be helpful, but it is by no means a complete answer, and there seems to be no solution to this problem that is entirely satisfactory.

Another problem prevalent at the moment in American colleges concerns the shortage of qualified women teachers and the effect on women of the tenure system. The attempt to have women represented adequately on various policy-making committees inevitably cuts into the time available to them to further their own scholarship. Yet when issues of tenure arise, they will suffer if scholarship has been neglected. They are caught between the immediate demand for input into the policy-making apparatus and the demand for career advancement, which in the long-run may provide them with greater opportunities for leadership. Presumably this dilemma will be resolved by the employment of greater numbers of women in organizations. But the persistence of such problems only underlines the need for the institution to make career advancement opportunities more flexible.

Colleges have been urged to offer curriculum courses that focus on women's contribution to all spheres of life. Many colleges have responded by adding a special course to an established department; others have initiated a major in Women's Studies. The particular method of incorporating such studies in the curriculum is less important than some recognition that women have assayed and succeeded in a variety of roles, many of which call for traits and talents very different from the stereotyped "feminine" attributes.

Over and above these curriculum adjustments, a different kind of learning could be explored by experiment. To gain a real grasp of the issues, both women and men students need to be directly exposed to various occupations and life styles. Margaret Mead has suggested that women undergraduates be provided with *internships in families* and, if her suggestion were followed, similar internships should certainly also be provided for men. American college students who have been attached as part of their education to foreign families have enlarged their attitudes and expanded their knowledge of variations in family life. The term *internship* may be too pretentious, but some such exposure in depth to another life style seems to have particular merit during this current transitional period when new possibilities in marital relationships are being explored.

The observations, research or internships here envisaged could all be linked to the more traditional classroom learning, vivifying the latter in the process. But observation and research in themselves offer limited experiences for learning, and undergraduates might be involved personally in experiment and innovation. For example, they might begin by studying a particular business organization or city government, assess the roles assigned to women in the structure under study, and then proceed to make recommendations for better utilization of women by the creation of new roles or even new occupations. Such a study would be incomplete without follow-up observations on what happens as a result of their recommendations. This is action research and a much needed style of learning. Similar projects could be related specifically to theories of child-rearing and linked directly to child-study programs already in existence at many colleges.

These suggestions imply a conception of the college enlarged in two directions: (1) in that of relating its undergraduate work more closely than at present to the problems of society and their solutions; and (2) in that of shaping the total development of the person, which thus becomes a much more deliberate focus of attention—not just for the sake of "enhancing the quality of life for the individual," but for the sake of providing the incentive for cognitive development, now so often lacking in the curriculum, by relating intellectual activity directly to aspects of the student's own life.

On a more mundane level, colleges must provide the same adjunct facilities for women that they provide for men, whether in athletics, health, or career counseling, and these facilities must take into account the differences between men and women. Although there are times when policies, laws, services or attitudes can be appropriately gender-blind, women have some unique needs, for example, gynecological services. Similarly, some differences will occur in athletic preferences and needs and in career advising, which still must accommodate to the fact that, if a child is to be born, it will be borne by the woman. Sex counseling is a service which is desirable for both sexes, but special counseling may be required for contraceptive methods that are female-related. The college psychiatrist can help both men and women through individual counseling and by advising faculty and administration on institutional policies that may alter restrictive attitudes toward women and increase the number of options open to them. Furthermore, colleges can experiment with housing alternatives, which may enhance women's confidence in themselves, as one study of co-residency has recently suggested.[25]

Finally, there must be some institutions which will undertake quite radical attempts to vary the patterns of education. Recently, Barbara Newell, President of Wellesley, spoke about a plan to offer admission to a significant number of women in the middle years, women whose child-bearing and child-rearing years were behind them. A few colleges and professional schools "without walls" have been established with the objective of making attendance more possible for, although not limited to, women who have time to study but find it difficult to leave home on a regularly scheduled basis. Perhaps an upgrading of correspondence courses could be attempted with a similar student body in mind. In this connection, the rapid development of cable TV could provide the vehicle for classroom instruction while making possible the collection of tuition fees. Such measures will only be effective, however, if they are able to avoid the tendency to equate the fact of being "for women" with being second-rate.

Changes in social values

The prospect of radical and rapid change of social values in a society as complex as that of the United States is perhaps an illusion. Yet it is necessary to stress that men have clearly been the dominant sex, and therefore many of the dominant values have been traditionally male values. Historically, the tendency of feminist movements has been to strive for the goal of equality (suffrage, equal job opportunity, pay, etc.). Understandably, thus far, the drive for equality has been associated with an acceptance of male values and the supposition that, if women are to take advantage of equal career opportunities, they will have to display the same aggressiveness, competitiveness and sometimes ruthlessness of their male colleagues.

The more far-reaching social change would be a shift in the system of values of the whole society, which would not necessarily reward these particular qualities but would also favor traditionally "feminine" qualities of cooperation, sensitivity and finesse. Even the concept of success might be redefined to the end that power or money or status was not necessarily the yardstick against which achievement is measured but rather service, and excellence of performance for its own sake.

Furthermore, in the pursuit of equality it is essential that many current administrative practices in organizations, both private and public, be changed to eliminate discrimination against women. Tax laws, insurance regulations and credit policies all currently distinguish between men and women, and almost without exception favor men in so doing. Such discrimination, while perhaps not central to the woman's dilemma, inevitably creates frustration, enhances feelings of low self-esteem, and significantly interferes with a woman's freedom of action.

REFERENCES

1. Gerhart Saenger. Minority Personality and Adjustment, *Transactions of the New York Academy of Science* 14 (1952): 204-208.

2. John P. McKee & Alex C. Sherriffs. The Differential Evaluation of Males and Females, *Journal of Personality* 25, 3 (1957): 356-371.

3. Alex C. Sherriffs & John P. McKee. Qualitative Aspects of Beliefs about Men and Women, *Journal of Personality* 25 (1957): 450-464.

4. Kenneth Keniston. "Themes and Conflicts of Autonomous Young Women," 19th Karen Horney Memorial Lecture presented at a meeting of the Association for the Advancement of Psychoanalysis in New York City March 24, 1971. Unpublished.

5. Alice S. Rossi. "The Roots of Ambivalence in American Women," in READINGS ON THE PSYCHOLOGY OF WOMEN, Judith M. Bardwick, Ed. (New York: Harper & Row, 1972) Chapter 18, pp 125-127.

6. Anne Steinmann, J. Levi & D. Fox. Self Concept of College Women Compared with Their Concept of Ideal Woman, *Journal of Consulting Psychology* 11 (1964): 370-374.

7. Keniston, *op. cit.*

8. *Ibid.*

9. *Idem.*

10. Anne Steinmann, J. Levi & D. Fox. Male-Female Perceptions of the Female Role in the United States, *Journal of Psychology* 64 (1966): 265-279.

11. Matina Horner. Fail: Bright Women, *Psychology Today* 3, 6 (1969): 36.

12. *Ibid.*

13. *Idem.*

14. Joseph Katz. "Coeducational Living: Effects upon Male-Female Relationships," in STUDENT DEVELOPMENT AND EDUCATION IN COLLEGE RESIDENCE HALLS, David A. Decoster & Phyllis L. Mable, Eds. (Washington, D.C.: American Personnel & Guidance Assn, 1974).

15. ——————. "Coeducational Living on Five College Campuses," 1972. Unpublished.

16. Rhona Rapoport & Robert N. Rapoport. The Dual Career Family, *Human Relations* 22 (1969): 3-30.

17. Lynda Lytle Holmstrom. "The Two-Career Family," address prepared for the Conference, "Women: Resource for a Changing World," Radcliffe Institute (Cambridge, Mass.: Radcliffe College, April 1972).

18. Rapoport & Rapoport, *op. cit.*

19. Holmstrom, *op. cit.*

20. Paul S. Rosenkrantz. "Egalitarian Families: Some Clinical Observations," address prepared for the Conference, "Women: Resource for a Changing World," Radcliffe Institute (Cambridge, Mass.: Radcliffe College, April 1972).

21. Nena O'Neill & George O'Neill. OPEN MARRIAGE (New York: Avon Books, 1972).

22. Eugene E. Levitt & Albert D. Klassen, Jr. Public Attitudes toward Sexual Behaviors: The Latest Investigation of the Institute for Sex Research, *American Journal of Orthopsychiatry* 43 (1973): 285-286.

23. Katz, "Coeducational Living: Effects upon Male-Female Relationships," *op. cit.*

24. Zella Luria. Recent Women College Graduates: A Study of Rising Expectations, *American Journal of Orthopsychiatry* 44 (1974): 312-327.

25. Elizabeth Aub Reid. Effects of Coresidential Living on the Attitudes, Self-Image, and Role Expectations of College Women, *American Journal of Psychiatry* 131 (1974): 551-554.

8

CONCLUSIONS AND RECOMMENDATIONS

The foregoing delineates the very real problems facing the college woman—and man—in universities and in society today. We have examined some of the influences that shape the internal attitudes of women, some of the external factors that impinge on their choices, and the consequences of these choices. We have identified attitudes, practices and policies that we believe should be changed by policy-making members of the University and the society, including mental health professionals. The Committee's most difficult task has been to describe these changes and how they could be effected. In making recommendations we have tried to keep in mind that colleges vary greatly from one to another, and that we could not be narrowly prescriptive. Furthermore, we recognized that a fundamental problem influencing both internal barriers and external factors is the attitude of society, which inevitably changes only slowly and against tremendous inertia. This is almost as true for complex institutions, which most of our colleges and universities are. Nevertheless, recognition of the problem is an essential first step, and a willingness to consider change a very crucial next step if change is to occur.

There are six major changes that the Committee on the College Student would like to see happen, three in the sphere of personal relationships and three in the institutional sphere:

1) A more open definition of femininity and masculinity
2) An emphasis on individual autonomy rather than adaptation to sex-role stereotypes as a definition of maturity

3) An acceptance of variations in traditional male-female relationships, marital patterns, and child-rearing practices, with a reflection of this acceptance spelled out in institutional attitudes and practices

4) An increased flexibility in both faculty and student arrangements for women

5) An increase in the number of women appointed to prominent university positions, to act as role models and to share their experience with college women (and men)

6) An attitude of "increased possibility" for women to participate significantly in all fields

Personal relationships

1) A more open definition of femininity and masculinity. The traditional definition of femininity involves passivity, submissiveness, intuitiveness and sensitivity, and as a corollary the avoidance of aggressiveness, competitiveness, rationality and logical thinking. If one adheres to this definition, a woman, no matter how educated, is at an almost insurmountable disadvantage in the pursuit of a career. It is therefore important, if the college or the society is serious about encouraging women to undertake roles other than those of housewife and mother, that this traditional definition be modified. Although these "feminine" qualities are traditionally associated with the capability for motherhood and wifehood, when scrutinized they do not really fit the woman for even those roles. Anyone who has attempted to run a household knows that many of the "nonfeminine" qualities are essential to success in domestic affairs as well as in a profession or a business. But when these qualities are exercised in the traditionally masculine world, they suddenly take on a different implication for both men and women. The woman who speaks up in the man's sphere is labeled "aggressive," a term having a particularly pejorative connotation when applied to the woman.

A necessary corollary to modification of the concept of femininity is modification of the traditional definition of masculinity. Many of the adjectives used to signify "feminine" require another person to complete their meaning and that other person is a man. Thus, the attribute of submissiveness implies submissiveness to a man, not a woman (although a dominant woman in relation to other women may be described as "a masculine woman"), and it requires dominance from the man to complete the dyad. Similarly, competitiveness often implies competition with a man. To a great extent the pressure for women to be "feminine" is that they be feminine in their relation to men, who supposedly see a threat to their "masculinity" if there is any shift in the balance of the traditional male-female relationship. If men could be less rigid in their definition of masculinity, and if they could accept the fact that they do not have to display traditional masculine qualities in every interpersonal transaction, a greater range of behavior without anxiety on the part of either sex would become possible.

2) An emphasis on individual autonomy. The most significant contribution of psychiatry to human growth and development has been to encourage the attainment of ego autonomy. Ego autonomy is a highly complex concept that defies simple definition, but roughly it relates to the individual's ability to control his or her life by adaptive choice and independent action. Ego autonomy assumes the inner freedom to develop one's potential both emotionally and intellectually. It implies the capacity to evaluate reality factors in the process of making choices, but does *not* mean simply "adjusting" to the *status quo* or to a specified social milieu. As we define it, ego autonomy calls for the ability to accept interdependency with other individuals and in the process to benefit from these dependencies rather than be crippled by them. Necessarily there will be differences in definitions of ego autonomy and the most abstract definition is a rather Utopian one, but it can serve as a

guide in avoiding some of the pitfalls present in the simplistic
dichotomies that are often used to describe its characteristics.
In the opinion of this committee, the one principle to be
observed above all others is that the individuality of every
person is to be valued and valiantly defended when under
attack by pressures for conformity or rigidity of role. This is
not an endorsement of simply "doing your own thing" but is
aimed at stressing the options available during any person's
development, especially that of young women, who, the
committee feels, are particularly burdened by the excess bag-
gage of rigid institutional and societal expectations.

**3) Acceptance of variations in male-female relationships and
child-rearing practices.** Dual-career families, egalitarian marriages, and partial or complete role reversal in parenting are
relatively new concepts of family living that are being tried by
couples today. Although it is too soon to assess the viability of
such variations on the marital theme, it is imperative to be
open to such experiments if the first two recommendations
are to be accepted. Many couples will prefer the traditional
male-female role relationship in marriage, and this
committee's recommendation for openness does not militate
against this pattern. The woman who finds fulfillment in the
role of wife and mother—and there are many—should not be
forced into another pattern in order to conform to feminist
ideology. To believe that one *must* combine marriage and
career is just as limiting as the belief that one must be solely a
homemaker. On the other hand, the woman who sees
homemaking as only a partial answer to self-realization, or
who sees it as a time-limited period in a broader life plan, may
require a different marital pattern, and it is to these women,
who currently have fewer guideposts, that much of this discussion is addressed. Furthermore, there may be both women
and men who eschew formal marriage and work out satisfactory interpersonal relationships while remaining single.

In regard to child-rearing, we have been through a century during which every advance in medicine and psychology has inspired another prescriptive formula as to how children should be raised in order to guarantee their physical and mental health. But we have arrived at a time when there is much less certainty—or at least agreement—about the "right" way of raising children. This diversity of opinion has evoked a more varied approach, partly as a consequence of disillusion with the authorities of the past and partly in response to the changing needs and goals of individual parents. Further research should be directed toward observing the results of these variations rather than be designed to press for conformity to some unitary ideological system.

The institutional sphere

4) Increased flexibility in faculty and student arrangements. There are women who manage full-time careers without serious conflict. Some choose to forego marriage and family. Others have the energy and resources to combine family and career commitments successfully. Whichever path women choose, they confront conflicts which men do not. Today's college students are trying to work out patterns of study, life and work which will enable both men and women to assume family responsibilities and at the same time discharge long-range career commitments. They are questioning the intense competitiveness, the success syndrome, and the sixty-plus hours per week taken for granted in many occupations. In trying to work out new patterns, they encounter inflexible institutional policies and structures that present formidable barriers. Frequently part-time work or study opportunities are either unavailable or available only at a sacrifice of quality. Child care resources are either inadequate or lacking altogether. Many regulations are specifically designed to discourage interruptions in curriculum.

In many other ways colleges have not adapted to the fact that students may be married and already have family concerns. Counseling services are needed to help young men and women cope with changing family roles because such changes pose real problems for both sexes. It can be argued that students "don't have to get married," but the fact is that many do marry, and in a society which values this kind of individual freedom of choice, the institutions of that society must recognize that policies adequate in the past no longer meet today's needs and will certainly not be appropriate for the future. Much trauma for individuals, for families, and for children yet to be born will result if institutions adhere rigidly to tradition instead of finding ways to make institutional goals compatible with the configurations of rapidly changing social patterns. Increased flexibility and a greater variety of options will undoubtedly benefit men as well as women, although the most urgent pressure is unquestionably felt by the latter.

5) An increase in the number of women appointed to university positions. The dearth of women holding prominent faculty and administrative positions in academic and professional settings who could serve as models and provide sources of identification is glaringly apparent. In the absence of such models, women students find it difficult to project themselves into the future in some career role or to believe they will find career opportunities after they develop specific interests. Furthermore, the absence of such models also handicaps men, who would have the opportunity to relate to women as colleagues, not only as mothers or wives. In our culture there is a general expectation that aspects of family life for both women and men are to be brought into the consideration of career plans. This creates special stresses and problems for women students, yet little effort is made to come to terms with the loss to the professions when talented women do not embark on some course of training or do not complete their training because of the barriers they encounter along the way.

In most educational settings little thought is given to the working out of program flexibility for the student (woman or man) even when the needs or interests of that student suggest some educational plan other than the traditional.

Given the socialization process, it is perhaps not surprising that so many women accept this situation as a *fait accompli* and express so little anger about it. Their reaction probably can be explained as a continuation of the adaptive process developed earlier in life as a means of getting along in school. But the anger is frequently present and often it erupts later after the full impact of the compromised situation has been felt. This aspect of the problem emphasizes the woman student's needs for counseling services, peer contacts, and role models, especially in schools with few women students, faculty members or administrators. Until recently, women felt that they should receive no special consideration on the basis of sex, and communication with other women was scorned. In the current atmosphere of feminist activity, many women are rediscovering the importance of providing support for one another and the value of obtaining information from women who have found different solutions for a common problem.

6) An increased possibility for women to participate in all fields. Both the college and the society must adopt an attitude of "increased possibility" for women to attempt and to succeed in any role. Although there have been recent attempts to make it possible for a woman to feel that she can enter any field, old attitudes die hard and many prejudices come to the surface when a woman does inquire about entering a hitherto male-dominated field. Thus, although there have been occasional woman surgeons for decades, a career in surgery for a woman is still considered sufficiently unusual that the woman is often discouraged from undertaking training. Such discouragement may take the form of a "realistic" description, usually by a male, of the difficulties of a career in that field. This would be reasonable enough, except for the fact that the majority of difficulties cited apply equally to men, but men are expected to be able to deal with adversity as part of their working life, whereas women are to be "protected."

Sometimes discouragement takes the cruder form of describing the hostility the woman will meet, which presumably will interfere with eventual success. This approach takes a more subtle form when the "discourager" does not question the woman's ultimate success but poses the question, "Why subject yourself to so much unpleasantness when you don't have to?" Indeed, this is a particularly difficult argument to counter because it encompasses some truth. Many if not all careers involve work that is either boring or unpleasant or both, and it is reasonable to avoid such work where possible. Omitted, however, from the argument are both the gratifications that may derive from a career and the potential "unpleasantness" involved in the alternative to a career.

These attitudes are also expressed gratuitously within the college in a myriad of guises. Sometimes it is the President who refers to "our beautiful coeds," thereby suggesting that beauty is their major contribution to college life. More significantly, these attitudes appear in the practices of career counseling offices, which have been organized primarily to advise male students on their way to business or industry. This committee does not consider it essential for the college to recruit women to fields in which they have no interest, but it is essential that, once interest is expressed, it be encouraged to the same extent that a similar interest by a man would be encouraged.

Summary

The college woman of today faces a future marked by uncertainty, difficulty, and probably some frustration—but one that also extends a hitherto nonexistent range of options and possibilities. Excitement, opportunity and creativity are available to her, but she must contend with external forces of inflexibility, reaction, and at times naked hostility, as well as with internal obstacles grounded in her own learned responses to stereotyped gender roles. Thus, the one experience that we can guarantee her is conflict. But we believe, perhaps only slightly overoptimistically, that through conflict can come growth. We do not expect that all women will find utopian solutions. Some may be miserable, and for many the availability of choice adds a further burden. Nevertheless, the changes which have begun to be influential in the last few years hold forth real hope to women that they will be able to use their education creatively. Finally, we believe that these changes can lead to greater fulfillment for a greater number of women than ever before, and, as a corollary, should also enhance the fulfillment of men.

FOR FURTHER READING

Anthony, James & Therese Benedek. PARENTHOOD: ITS PSYCHOLOGY AND PSYCHOPATHOLOGY (Boston: Little, Brown, 1970).

Astin, Helen S. THE WOMAN DOCTORATE IN AMERICA (New York: Russell Sage Foundation, 1970).

Astin, Helen S., Nancy Suniewick & Susan Dweck. WOMEN: A BIBLIOGRAPHY ON THEIR EDUCATION AND CAREERS (Washington, D.C.: Human Service Press, 1971).

Bardwick, Judith M. THE PSYCHOLOGY OF WOMEN (New York: Harper & Row 1971).

—————, Ed. READINGS IN THE PSYCHOLOGY OF WOMEN (New York: Harper & Row, 1972).

Bernard, Jessie. ACADEMIC WOMEN (University Park, Pa.: Pennsylvania State University Press, 1964).

—————. THE FUTURE OF MARRIAGE (New York: World Publishing, 1972).

Bullough, Vern L. & Bonnie Bullough. THE SUBORDINATE SEX (Baltimore: Penguin Books, 1974).

Cade, Toni, Ed. THE BLACK WOMAN (New York: New American Library, 1970).

Carnegie Commission on Higher Education. OPPORTUNITIES FOR WOMEN IN HIGHER EDUCATION (New York: McGraw-Hill, 1973).

Chafe, William H. THE AMERICAN WOMAN (New York: Oxford University Press, 1972).

Cornillon, Susan K., Ed. IMAGES OF WOMEN IN FICTION: FEMINIST PERSPECTIVES (Bowling Green, Ohio: Bowling Green Press, 1972).

Epstein, Cynthia Fuchs. WOMAN'S PLACE (Berkeley, Calif.: University of California Press, 1971).

Farber, Seymour M. & Roger H.L. Wilson, Eds. MAN AND CIVILIZATION: THE POTENTIAL OF WOMAN; a symposium (New York: McGraw-Hill, 1963).

Firestone, Shulamith. THE DIALECTIC OF SEX (New York: Morrow, 1970).

Franks, Violet & Vasanti Burtle. WOMEN IN THERAPY (New York: Brunner/Mazel, 1974).

Fuller, Margaret. WOMEN IN THE NINETEENTH CENTURY (New York: W.W. Norton, 1971).

Ginzberg, Eli & Alice M. Yohalem, Eds. CORPORATE LIB: WOMEN'S CHALLENGE TO MANAGEMENT (Baltimore, Md.: Johns Hopkins University Press, 1973).

Gornick, Vivian & Barbara K. Moran, Eds. WOMAN IN SEXIST SOCIETY (New York: Signet Books, 1972).

Greer, Germaine. THE FEMALE EUNUCH (New York: Bantam Books, 1972).

Group for the Advancement of Psychiatry. SEX AND THE COLLEGE STUDENT (New York: Fawcett World Library, 1966).

Grunebaum, Henry & Jacob Christ, Eds. MARRIAGE: PROBLEMS AND PROSPECTS (Boston: Little, Brown, 1974).

Huber, Joan, Ed. CHANGING WOMEN IN A CHANGING SOCIETY (Chicago: University of Chicago Press, 1973).

Janeway, Elizabeth: MAN'S WORLD, WOMEN'S PLACE (New York: Dell Publishing, 1972).

Jencks, Christopher & David Riesman. THE ACADEMIC REVOLUTION (Garden City, N.Y.: Anchor Books, Doubleday, 1969).

Kraditor, Aileen S., Ed. UP FROM THE PEDESTAL (Chicago: Quadrangle Books, 1968).

Kreps, Juanita. SEX IN THE MARKETPLACE: AMERICAN WOMEN AT WORK (Baltimore, Md.: Johns Hopkins University Press, 1971).

Kundsin, Ruth, Ed. WOMEN & SUCCESS (New York: William Morrow, 1974).

Lifton, Robert Jay, Ed. THE WOMAN IN AMERICA (Boston: Beacon Press, 1967).

Maccoby, Eleanor E., Ed. THE DEVELOPMENT OF SEX DIFFERENCES (Stanford, Calif.: Stanford University Press, 1966).

Masters, William H. & Virginia E. Johnson. HUMAN SEXUAL RESPONSE (Boston: Little, Brown, 1966).

Mead, Margaret. MALE AND FEMALE (New York: William Morrow, 1949).

Mill, John Stuart & Harriet Taylor Mill. ESSAYS ON SEXUAL EQUALITY, Alice S. Rossi, Ed. (Chicago: University of Chicago Press, 1970).

Miller, Jean Baker, Ed. PSYCHOANALYSIS AND WOMEN (Baltimore: Penguin Books, 1973).

Millett, Kate. SEXUAL POLITICS (New York: Avon Books, 1971).

Mitchell, Juliet. PSYCHOANALYSIS AND FEMINISM (New York: Pantheon Books, 1974).

—————. WOMEN'S ESTATE (New York: Vintage Books, 1973).

Money, John & Anke A. Ehrhardt. MAN & WOMAN, BOY & GIRL (Baltimore, Md.: Johns Hopkins University Press, 1972).

Morgan, Robin, Ed. SISTERHOOD IS POWERFUL (New York: Vintage Books, 1970).

Nye, F. Ivan & Lois W. Hoffman, Eds. THE EMPLOYED MOTHER IN AMERICA (Chicago: Rand McNally & Co., 1963).

Rapoport, Rhona & Robert N. Rapoport. DUAL CAREER FAMILIES (Baltimore: Penguin Books, 1971).

Reid, Inez Smith. "TOGETHER" BLACK WOMEN (New York: Emerson Books, 1972).

Rosenbaum, Salo & Ian Alger, Eds. THE MARRIAGE RELATIONSHIP (New York: Basic Books, 1968).

Rossi, Alice S., Ed. THE FEMINIST PAPERS (New York: Bantam Books, 1974).

Schaeffer, Dirk L., Ed. SEX DIFFERENCES IN PERSONALITY READINGS (Belmont, Calif.: Brooks/Cole, 1971).

Sherfey, Mary Jane. THE NATURE AND EVOLUTION OF FEMALE SEXUAL-ITY (New York: Vintage Books, 1973).

Stoller, Robert J. SEX AND GENDER (New York: Science House, 1968).

Symposium, "Women: Resource for a Changing World," Radcliffe Institute, April 1972 (Cambridge, Mass. 02138: Radcliffe College, 1972).

Westervelt, Esther Manning & Deborah A. Fixter. WOMEN'S HIGHER AND CONTINUING EDUCATION: AN ANNOTATED BIBLIOGRAPHY WITH SELECTED REFERENCES ON RELATED ASPECTS OF WOMEN'S LIVES (New York: College Entrance Examination Board, 1971).

Zubin, Joseph & John Money, Eds. CONTEMPORARY SEXUAL BEHAVIOR: CRITICAL ISSUES IN THE 1970's (Baltimore: Johns Hopkins University Press, 1973).

Some psychoanalytic writings

Chasseguet-Smirgel, Janine. FEMALE SEXUALITY (Ann Arbor, Mich.: University of Michigan Press, 1970).

Deutsch, Helene. PSYCHOLOGY OF WOMEN, Vol. I, Girlhood Vol. II, Motherhood (New York: Bantam Books, 1973).

Erikson, Erik: CHILDHOOD AND SOCIETY (New York: W. W. Norton, 1963).

_____ . IDENTITY AND THE LIFE CYCLE Psychological Issues (New York: International Universities Press, 1959).

_____ . IDENTITY: YOUTH AND CRISIS (New York: W. W. Norton, 1968).

Freud, Anna. THE EGO AND THE MECHANISMS OF DEFENSE (London: Hogarth Press, 1942).

Freud, Sigmund. NEW INTRODUCTORY LECTURES ON PSYCHOANAL-YSIS, James Strachey. Ed. (New York: W. W. Norton, 1965)

_____ . SEXUALITY AND THE PSYCHOLOGY OF LOVE, Philip Rieff, Ed. (New York: Collier Books, 1963).

Horney, Karen. FEMININE PSYCHOLOGY, Harold Kelman, Ed. (New York: W. W. Norton, 1973).

ACKNOWLEDGMENTS TO CONTRIBUTORS

The program of the Group for the Advancement of Psychiatry, a nonprofit, tax-exempt organization, is made possible largely through the voluntary contributions and efforts of its members. For their financial assistance during the past fiscal year in helping it to fulfill its aims, GAP is grateful to the following:

Sponsors

J. Aron Charitable Foundation
CIBA-GEIGY Corporation, Pharmaceuticals Division
The Division Fund
Maurice Falk Medical Fund
The Grove Foundation
The Holzheimer Fund
Ittleson Family Foundation
Merck, Sharp & Dohme Laboratories
The Olin Foundation
Pfizer Laboratories
The Phillips Foundation
Roche Laboratories
Rockefeller Brothers Fund
Sandoz Pharmaceuticals
Schering Corporation
The Murray L. Silberstein Fund
The Lucille Ellis Simon Foundation
Smith, Kline & French Laboratories
E. R. Squibb & Sons
The Sunnen Foundation
van Ameringen Foundation, Inc.
Leo S. Weil Foundation
Lawrence Weinberg
Weyerhaeuser Foundation, Inc.
Wyeth Laboratories

Donors

Fannie & Arnold Askin Foundation
Mrs. Walter H. Etzbach
Orrin Stine
The Stone Foundation, Inc.

OTHER PUBLICATIONS OF INTEREST
GROUP FOR THE ADVANCEMENT OF PSYCHIATRY

No.	Title	Price
60	SEX AND THE COLLEGE STUDENT	$1.50
52	THE COLLEGE EXPERIENCE: A FOCUS FOR PSYCHIATRIC RESEARCH......................................	1.00
68	NORMAL ADOLESCENCE: ITS DYNAMICS AND IMPACT...	1.65
86	HUMANE REPRODUCTION....................................	4.00
84	THE JOYS AND SORROWS OF PARENTHOOD............	4.00

Orders amounting to less than $5.00 must be accompanied by remittance. All prices are subject to change without notice.

GAP publications may be ordered on a subscription basis. The current subscription cycle comprising the Volume IX Series covers the period from July 1, 1974 to June 30, 1977. For further information, write the Publications Office (see below).

Bound volumes of GAP publications issued since 1974 are also available which include GAP titles no longer in print and no longer available in any other form. A bound index to these volumes (I through VII) has been published separately.

Please send your order and remittance to: Publications Office, Group for the Advancement of Psychiatry, 419 Park Avenue South, New York, New York 10016.

This publication was produced for the Group for the Advancement of Psychiatry by the Mental Health Materials Center, Inc., New York.